mini comas

ISBN: 1495461688
ISBN 13: 9781495461682
Library of Congress Control Number: 2014902872
CreateSpace Independent Publishing Platform
North Charleston, South Carolina

Dedication

To my wife Ana, sons David and Michael and daughter-in-law Damaris who don't roll their eyes at my sense of humor. To my grandson Xavier who I consider the bestest of the bestest and who shares the same mental age as I (well maybe he is a few years older)

Lastly, to Gretchen from Createspace who edited the book and, although she is paid, appeared to think the book was funny which makes six all together excluding myself because I'm biased. Well, come to think of it, so is everyone else.

Mini Comas and Other Odd Thoughts

WILLIAM R. HANSON

Contents

I Discover I Am Comatose

I have been aware for some time that big changes are happening all around me. I seem to be totally oblivious to them, until one day I say, "What the hey? When did that happen?" Bam, there it is, and I never saw it coming.

Sometimes I wonder if I've somehow gotten caught in an Ionesco play, where logic is suspended and nothing makes much sense. Or maybe I'm trapped in a Fellini film like *Satyricon*, where odd people do odd things and I'm not getting any of it. Sometimes I kind of feel like the dinosaurs: one day I'm munching on lush tropical foliage or the flesh of some other dinosaur, and the next, the mammals are moving in. If it all happened like Darwinian evolution—you know, humanoids walking on all fours at a very slow pace, finally getting a backache, and then standing up after a few million years— that would be fine, but no. These things are just there. Yesterday they weren't, and today, there they are.

But you know, I finally put my finger on it...It seems to me that what is happening to me are "mini comas." I black out while things are going on around me, and then one day it hits me. I wake up to see that the world has changed in some major way.

In everyday life, the concept of mini comas goes something like this. Let's suppose that your wife decides to change out the sofa in your living room with something made with bamboo (especially in South Florida). Now prior to this, you have been dragged to many stores by your wife and probably never noticed bamboo furniture at all. But now that your wife wants a bamboo sofa,

1

you notice the stuff is everywhere you look. Every store has it, but you just never noticed it. You, my friend, have just encountered the bamboo coma. One minute there wasn't any bamboo furniture and the next minute it is all around you. So, without further ado, I've decided to describe a few of the many mini comas I've experienced over the years. Feel free to add your own.

Freaking Fat Coma

I awoke from what I call the "freaking fat coma" while I was in a Walmart parking lot in New Philadelphia, Ohio. I was visiting my mom, and for some reason I had a crying need to go to Walmart to buy something or other.

Any who, I made a stop at the local Walmart, and while I was walking in, I spied this enormous woman waddling toward the door. I was totally baffled—this woman was enormous. She could have fed an African country for some years. Her legs were so big and fat that I found it hard to believe she could walk without creating enough friction to set herself ablaze.

I looked around to see how she had gotten there. I had visions of someone slathering her in pounds of melted butter with a huge pastry brush just to squeeze her into some car, or putting a giant shoehorn under her butt to shove her in. Or else someone had come up with a ray to shrink her down so she would fit into a car. (I discounted this soon after, as this would be the same as putting a black hole in the trunk of your car: way too dense.)

Or maybe they used a forklift and deposited her onto some half-ton truck and then drove to Walmart, but then where was the forklift to unload her at this end? Did Walmart supply one?

Maybe she didn't live that far away and someone had rolled her there. I briefly considered Star Trek-style teleporting, but decided against that. That machine had enough trouble getting ordinary people straight. Can you imagine it decoding then encoding that much blubber? It would take years to get her anywhere.

Anyway, she makes it through the door, huffing and puffing, and this is when I really had my awakening. Obviously, one grossly overweight person doesn't mean much, but once she got into the store, I heard her arguing with a clerk:

Clerk:

> I am sorry, ma'am, but we had an electrical problem last night and the electric carts aren't working.

I looked toward where they were pointing. I had never realized it before, but this Walmart had no fewer than ten electric carts. My jaw dropped. This was New Philly, population of 17,000 or so, but one Walmart had this many electric carts? I was staggered. Now, either there was an epidemic of heart problems in good old New Philadelphia, Ohio, or most of these carts were for people like her.

The anesthetic had worn off now, and I was fully conscious of the fact that somehow, people had gotten really fat. Not pudgy, or rotund, or "healthy," as my ma used to say, but hugely fat.

I came out of my reverie to hear the following conversation:

> "So what am I supposed to do?" said the fat lady sneeringly. "I need a cart".

> "I am very sorry, ma'am, but as I said, none of the carts are working at this time." repeated the clerk.

The fat lady humphed and marched (well, waddled) out of the store. I have no idea where she was going from there. I assume she had to call the half-ton truck to come and pick her up.

Freaking Fat Coma

Okay, okay, one store, a bunch of carts, and one fat person. Maybe not that big of a problem. But later in the week, I was in the same store (apparently I can't stay away from Walmart) and there was this gargantuan woman on a cart. Her whole body was draped over it, such that you actually had trouble seeing the cart. I'm telling you, if that cart were a burro or a mule; she'd be up on charges for animal cruelty.

So old Jabba the Hut is wheeling around the store with her family, and I am really wondering how they got her there. This is beyond slathered butter or a giant shoehorn. I can only imagine how the pyramids were made, but somehow they were, and likewise, this woman's family had somehow magically gotten her to Walmart.

And the really amazing thing was that she was really angry about how tight the aisles were. I couldn't believe it.

How could anyone let themselves get this fat? Growing up, I don't remember seeing anyone that heavy. Sure there were fat people, but not what we call now morbidly obese. Not only was she hugely fat but she had to use an electric cart, which, by the by, I don't remember either growing up, and she was complaining about the narrowness of the aisles to boot.

Okay, okay, a couple of trips to Walmart and some morbidly obese people, so what? How about this?:

I'm at Islands of Adventure in Orlando, Florida, and outside the Dudley Do-Right river raft ride, they have placed one of the ride's log cars outside for people to see. Above the car is a sign, which says, "If you can't fit into this car, you won't be able to get on the ride."

So this tells me that between the time Dudley Do-Right became a cartoon (if you are that old), the time Islands of Adventure decided to make a ride out it, and today, people have become so fat that they actually have to have you try to get your fat ass in the car before you can attempt to get on the ride.

I'd like it better if the people taking your ticket would just say, "You are too damn fat to get on the ride." Or maybe they should set up a cutout of a person and if you can't fit your fat ass through the opening, you can't get on. I'm

5

amazed The Islands of Adventure haven't been sued to build a bigger ride to support these people.

Later that same day, I'm waiting to go on the Spiderman ride when I see this enormous person in an electric cart, leaning back on his seat with a baby perched on his chest.

I thought about running over to scoop up the child in case he was going to slurp her down like any other amusement park fare.

And get this, since my coma lasted we had become so fat that in New York City they train special EMT personnel on procedures for extricating an obese person from their apartment should they not be able to get out. Wow, double wow.

Or how about this? I remember another story where this cruise boat capsized in some lake and a bunch of the people onboard drowned. The boat had a limit of 48 people allowed on board based on a calculation of weight per person in the 1960s, but today those same 48 people weighed much more than they did then which contributed to the capsizing of the boat. Wow! Again how did this happen? I didn't see it coming until I went to Walmart years later.

What happened? How did we get so fat? Is it simply the effects of fast food? Oh no, my friend. There is much more to it than that.

Personally, I think lawyers bear the most responsibility for the fat epidemic. There was a time when you had to take gym in school; you had to run and jump, and do this or that, or you failed. Well, Johnny doesn't have to do that anymore. Lawyers made sure of that.

"You can't fail Johnny just 'cause he's a fat slob," they say. "We will sue your ass". Poor, fat Johnny; it isn't his fault. It's society's fault for imposing these fitness standards. Go ahead, Johnny, have another fry and a gross of Twinkies."

But you can't blame lawyers entirely, as much as I'd like to. It also has to do with TV and videogames. When I was growing up, my mom would toss us out and tell us to come back at sunset. She really didn't want to see us before that. We played army, we collected crawdads, we played kickball 'til dark. Not anymore; now everyone sits around and plays videogames all day. I say, let's sue Nintendo or Microsoft. This is their fault.

But you know, come to think of it, I do blame the lawyers. You can't just throw your kid outside anymore or you'll be arrested for child abuse. Plus, the media now have us convinced that there is a predator hiding behind every bush, so there's tremendous guilt in just throwing your child outdoors.

When I woke up from my fat coma, I suddenly realized that fat is big business. No one actually wants to see you lose a pound. Well, maybe Richard Simmons after you've purchased his *Sweatin' to the Oldies* and his dial-a-meal, but everyone else wants you fat. There's no money in thin.

90 percent of the ads on TV these days are for some kind of fat thing or another: fat pills, exercise equipment to get you un-fat, lip-smacking meals you can mail-order from Jenny Craig and Nutrisystem to lose weight.

Do you remember growing up with all this fatness on TV? I don't. I remember ads for Ipana toothpaste, Cheerios, Prell shampoo, and Anacin, with your head pounding like a hammer on an anvil, and an electric bolt, and Wisk to solve ring around the collar, or white sheets you could see from a balloon using some detergent or other. I don't remember fat-anything. And do you remember growing up with all these gyms around to get you un-fat? I remember gym in school, but that was about it.

Waist size is now irrelevant because clothing designers have compensated for our new fatness. Now when you buy Levi jeans, they now come with *relaxed fit* or *loose fit*. So if you were a size 38, you have probably moved on to a 42 from packing on the pounds, but Levi still calls you a size 38, relaxed fit. But what does that mean for the once-42? What size are you, really?

And forget about the gym and diets, the new thing is to staple your stomach to make you thin. I don't know about you but I find that totally creepy.

Am I the only one out there that thinks stapling your stomach should be the absolute last resort? But now it's common practice. Here's an incredibly dangerously procedure that no one knows the long-term effects of and everyone is doing it. Yikes. Are we totally mad? I don't know about you, but it seems to me that the famous folks who have had it done just get fat all over again.

The Hanson solution? Make cardboard and plastic bags taste good. Create cardboard that tastes like filet mignon or whatever else you like. Fill up on fiber and reduce the load headed for the landfill at the same time. Consider Caesar salad made from grocery stores' plastic bags. Hey, we already have processed food with a list of ingredients no one has heard of. Why not plastic bags? At least we know what we are getting and we are saving a dolphin or two in the bargain. Oh, shoot Nutrisystem already thought of it.

My other idea is to stop feeding the fat. Just like a bartender is legally responsible for your drinking problem, restaurants and grocery stores should be held accountable for people's eating problems. You should have to step on a scale when you go food shopping, and that would determine what food and how much of it you can buy.

And forget about asking your skinny neighbor for help on this front—we have that covered. You will be prosecuted for aiding and abetting a fat person, skinny neighbor, so even don't try it.

Tattoo Coma

I really believe that I blacked out for about a year. That's the only way I can explain how so many people managed to dance down to their local tattoo parlor and cover themselves with tattoos. Or maybe the tattoos came in the mail and people just slapped them on. I'm sure I didn't get one.

I remember working for my dad when I was younger, and there would be guys from WWII, especially navy guys, with maybe an anchor or the occasional hula girl on their biceps, but that was about it. I really believe that this had been the state of affairs for most of my life, until the mini coma came on.

When I woke up, everyone had a tattoo, and not just one, but whole gobs of them. Not just young folks, but old folks with tattooed ankle bracelets.

Why? I don't get it. I mean, if you went in to see your doctor, and he rolled up his sleeves and you saw a map of Asia on his arm, would you be inclined to stick around? Sorry, not me. Maybe it's not fair, but I don't really trust anyone that has covered their bodies in tattoos. To me, having Tattoos says, "Hey, look at me! I want to be the CEO of a Wall Street firm, or maybe the head of some large bank." Nah, no it doesn't. Having tattoos says trailer park, sleeveless white shirt, a beer, and Wanda Sue cooking hot dogs on a grill obtained with Green Stamps.

Once upon a time, the police could use a tattoo to identify a lawbreaker. A bank would be robbed and the teller would say, "The robber had a tattoo of an anchor on his arm." Then the police would say, "Oh, that's Bob Andrews. Only guy I know with an anchor tattoo." Nope, can't do it anymore; everyone's got one.

And I wonder, who are they really for? Gone are the days of the carnival with the tattooed lady you could stare at. Are these tattoos for the benefit of the person that has them? Do they stand in front of a mirror and look them over at night, saying, "Wow, these are cool"? And what about the ones on your back? You'd need to stand with your back to a mirror while looking in another mirror to even see them.

Or are they for someone else to see and admire? I mean, I hardly even get the designs of most of them, and I imagine you wouldn't be able to stare at someone's tattoos for too long without looking kinda like a complete nutcase. And what happens when you get old and your eagle kinda looks more like a buzzard, and a wrinkly buzzard at that? It isn't gonna be pretty, my friend.

I will be very depressed the day my grandson is watching *Thomas the Tank Engine* and Thomas and Percy have tattoos on the side of their engines and rings in their noses. Maybe we'll even be seeing TV ads in the future for Tattoo Barbie.

Al-Qaeda Coma

We all know where we were when we woke up from this mini coma. I was in the office of Woods Network Services in Farmington, Connecticut, in the conference room, watching the planes hit the Twin Towers. I knew, as everyone did, that this was no accident. Someone had done this on purpose. 9/11 taught us about those jolly folks that were part of Al-Qaeda and the Taliban. Where did they come from? I certainly don't remember so many nut cases growing up. Did they spring from the sand somehow? My God, there hasn't been this kind of mayhem since the crusades.

I have a theory about the find folks who are members of Al-Qaeda and the Taliban. I believe they are really pod people from *Invasion of the Body Snatchers*. If you didn't catch the original or the remake, the idea is that these pods come from another planet and they take your place one by one until there is nothing left but pod people. I really can't think of any other rational explanation. They can't be real people unless someone slipped something in the water and totally eliminated all vestige of human decency. Another government experiment gone awry, I suppose.

The amazing thing is, if you catch one of these lovely pod people everything changes. They have this remarkable habit of going from ruthless killers to poor put upon victims. The first thing out of their mouths is,. "Whoa there, partner. Wait just a cotton pickin' minute. No one read me my Miranda rights."

There is really only one answer to these hilarious pod people. Our best scientists have to sit in a lab until they come up with a special dust. We cover tiny American flags with this new dust, and then use drones to drop the flags all over the Al-Qaeda and Taliban infested areas. Now, we know the pods will pick up the flags up and wave their fists in the air. But what does this dust do?

I'm glad you asked. It changes pod people into call center personnel asking how they can give the best customer experience to their clientele. It's perfect: we get rid of these nuts, and end up with people answering questions about medical and insurance claims. Of course, when you call in they will have names like Buffy and Dale Allen with very thick accents, but I think that is a small price to pay.

Wait a minute. This is brilliant. Forget about call center personnel. The dust turns males into females. That'll crimp their style don't you think?

Germ Coma

When did we get so damn germy? I don't remember growing up with my mother constantly spraying the air with some kind of germicide, or washing our hands twenty times a day. Now when you watch TV, you see these things crawling all over your counter and your phone unless you use some kind of spray.

Where did they come from? Are they from some alien planet? When did they arrive? Certainly not while I was growing up (maybe they didn't like Bakelite phones). I remember my mother saying, "Everyone must eat a peck of dirt before they die." That was the same as the five-second rule in her day.

One day we're pretty germ-free, and the next we're pulling wipes out of machines at grocery stores and wiping down the germ-laden carts. One day you're going to the gym and wiping our sweaty brows with a towel you brought from home, and the next, you're spritzing everything you can find. And damn if you don't fall into the trap.

Now when I'm on the treadmill at the gym and my neighbor gets off, but forgets to spray the whole thing down with some Gatorade or whatever that is, I say to myself, "That clod. How dare he?" when really what I should be saying is, "Good for you not falling for this goofiness." I challenge anyone to find someone who died as a direct result of using gym equipment someone didn't wipe off correctly.

And what about pets? Why aren't they wrapped in plastic wrap? Those tongues are lethal germ weapons. What about kissing? Should totally give that up. Wow, germs galore. And how about staying at one of those "less expensive" hotels. Don't go there. There are so many on your bedspread you can hear them discussing their plans for global domination

Personally, I think we should wallow in germs. The more germs, the better, if you ask me. Bring 'em on. Germs from different countries, germs of different races, ethnic germs, Democrat germs, Republican germs, Lawyer germs (no wait scratch that last one). The more the merrier, I say. The friendlier you get with your germs, the less likely anything is going to happen to you when you pick up the phone.

The germs will just say, "Can you make it snappy? We're expecting an important call."

Scam Coma

Somewhere along the line, I went into another mini coma, and when I awoke, I found that the level of scamdom had risen to such an extent that it makes your head swim. It is mindboggling to me how many ads on TV are for some worthless snake oil that will take the pounds off, or relieve your arthritic joints, or cure your lagging sex drive, or blow the mucus out of your head, or fix your constipation problems and convert you to a Democrat all at the same time.

Come on, folks. Wake up. These products don't work, they've never worked, and they are never going to work. The companies make their money on the initial bottle of worthless pills, plus the ridiculous shipping and handling. How do we keep falling for this stuff? How much fecal material do you really think there is in your bowels? These advertisers make you believe that you have several feet of the stuff.

Now, I had a colonoscopy. I was given this god-awful powder to mix with water and then spent a couple of hours in the bathroom, but I don't remember pounds of stuff coming out. So these companies would have me believe that when I went in for the procedure, I was still packed with the stuff.

But guess what? I don't remember the doctor coming up to me after the procedure and saying, "Mr. Hanson, do you know you are full of shit?"

"Why no, doctor, I had no idea."

"Yes, Mr. Hanson, but if you had been taking Colon-Shove, you wouldn't have this problem."

Or how about all those get-rich schemes? Most of them have to do with selling real estate and making a fortune. "You too could buy real estate at pennies on the dollar, if you only knew what I know. And you can know what I know by simply sending me $59.95, plus shipping and handling."

And then they interview all of these smiling folks who testify that in a few short months, they all quit their regular jobs, bought a Ferrari and a mansion in La Jolla, California, and now have a good-looking babe on each arm. I'd be smiling too if someone paid me to stand there and swear I had really made it, especially with two paid babes on my arms.

"Mr. Hanson, you fat slob, sign up for my diet pills and you'll lose weight like all of these fake people we pay to say how much weight they've lost."

"I lost fifty pounds on the fat-burning diet," a faker claims.

Of course, the said fat person was probably never fat ever or they were photoshopped to look thin or they were put in fat suits to make the commercial.

Doesn't it kill you that no matter how many experts point out the shortcomings of all this stuff, we continue to buy it anyway? But maybe that's the American way. Maybe this is capitalism at its best.

It would be nice if there was a way of making folks more skeptical, but I don't see it happening. If you're the kind who waits with bated breath to see Kim Kardashian's next tanning session, I don't see much hope.

Law Coma

The law coma really was more like a series of epileptic fits over the years. Remember when you were a kid and lawyers were the people your parents used to close on a house, or maybe look at some contract? Your parents would roll their eyes and call anything else they did "ambulance chasing."

I think the whole thing crystallized for me with class action suits. I suddenly realized that the legal profession is, for the most part, is legalized extortion.

Let's take class action suits. You get a thing in the mail about some stock in some tech company you may or may have not bought in the early '90s. Well dang if these companies didn't overestimate earnings or some such thing. What a shock. I'm flabbergasted. How could this have happened? Now I feel like gathering a crowd of townspeople with clubs and torches like in Frankenstein and going after the evil company.

The fact is, it didn't matter. We were all trading technology stocks day to day, and didn't give a hoot and a holler about whether they were making any money or not. That was irrelevant—their stock was going up.

But hold on. It's not my fault that I didn't read the company's balance sheet. It's not my fault that they really weren't doing anything useful. So now, twenty years later, if I can prove that I owned stocks in these companies and I can prove that I bought and sold between May 10th, 1992, and July 10, then I can participate.

Huh? Does anyone even have those kinds of records? Nope. Do the lawyers care? Nope. In fact, they are hoping you don't have any records because they really don't want to give you a cut of the extortion. That is what it is, clear and simple.

Some lawyer comes up with some bogus reason why some company didn't do something right, and they sue on behalf of us poor slobs. The company in question hands over a gob of money to the lawyers rather than fight it, without saying if they were guilty or innocent, just that they decided to settle. Any check in the mail to you? Of course not.

Let's face it folks, legalized extortion is what it is. You sue someone, the lawyer tells the defendant that he demands, say, $100,000, or else. The defendant, if it is a company of some sort, returns with a battery of their own lawyers with their own fish to fry, and who don't really want to drag this through court, so they say, "$20,000. The lawyer gets his third, you get your two-thirds, and that's that. Makes you proud to be an American.

Hey, I've got an idea. Let's start a mutual fund based off these lawyers' success in suing the ass off some company. We'll all buy shares and be participants. The more they get for these bogus suits, the more our shares of the mutual fund will be worth. It's fabulous, it can't miss. We will be rooting for ambulance chasers and their claims of wrong doing from asbestos, to vaginal mesh, to cigs, to drugs that have side effects (no tell me it ain't so). The better they do the more money we make. Is that the new American way or what?

I blame lawyers for practically everything that is wrong in the world today. First off, they have turned our minds to complete mush. They are not rational people (not Al-Qaeda evil pods but irrational pods), and we have fallen into their traps by believing the crap that stems from their thought processes. There used to be a time when two plus two equaled four, but now you can get a lawyer to argue that it depends on the state of the two and what is really meant by *two*. And the jury sits there and nods their heads.

They use unverified, unproven science based on the worst kind of speculation to make their cases and get away with it. They have made us a nation of whining victims who couldn't possibly be responsible for our own actions: "Hey, nobody told me you couldn't give yourself a haircut with a lawnmower. I didn't see that in the instructions."—"Hey, I didn't know you couldn't iron your shirt while you were wearing it. Where's that in the iron instructions?"

If you think I haven't made my case well enough, consider picking up the manual from one of your major appliances and giving it a read. Here are a few of the warnings that came with my Samsung fridge.

1. Do not insert the power plug with wet hands. (I'm trying to picture the nitwit who sued over this one: "Dang it, I always thought your hands should be sopping wet before plugging anything in. Now I know better.")
2. Do not store articles on top of the refrigerator. (I'm really glad to know this one, as I just removed the anvil I'd been storing up there.)
3. Do not let children enter inside the refrigerator. ("Hey, Dad, is it okay if I hop in the old fridge and shut the door?"—"Sure, son. I don't see any reason why not. Doesn't say anything against it in the manual.")
4. Do not spray flammable gas near the refrigerator. (For those of you who happen to be spraying flammable gas around your house, have at it anywhere else, but not in front of the fridge.)

You get the gist, and it goes on and on and on. And you know damn well why—some idiot did one of these things and then sued over it.

What amazes me is why these instructions aren't written in every known language. Wouldn't want to leave anyone out, after all. There must be someone out there that still speaks Aramaic who wouldn't understand.

If this were the case, I can just picture the manual that would come with every fridge. You'd need a forklift to get it into your car. It would list every known thing you can't do with a refrigerator in every known and unknown language. We would have teams of people who do nothing but sit around in a room and discuss what you can't do with a refrigerator. "It doesn't make a good coffin."—"Doesn't make an effective bookend."—"Can't use it as a surfboard." And on and on and on.

To save potential suers the trouble, I've got some other "don'ts" I think should be added to various products:

1. Do not stick your tongue in the toaster to test if your toast is done. I know there is probably a keen desire to do so, but refrain; it will not end well.

2. Do not strap a ladder to your back and jump off a cliff. A ladder does not make a good pair of wings. Odd, but true.
3. Paper shredders are not good for either manicures or pedicures. Unbelievable, but true.
4. Your pet will not get dry in a microwave. Astounding.

TV Coma

I guess I should have seen this coming. Like man making his way from monkey to man (and back again), there is fossil record of the evolution of one type of cretin to another. It started with shows like Jerry Springer.

I remember watching it and thinking, Please, God, let these people be paid actors. They can't be real people. But no—I was wrong. They all crawled out from under their respective rocks and slithered their way onto Jerry's show.

But I was hopeful that this sort of show was contained. It was a mini, tasteless flu that we could control. It wouldn't spread. It was like a nuclear plant with a minor leak. It could be contained as there were safety features in place to stop the spread. People were basically bright. People didn't really want to see too much of this garbage. People had taste.

Nope.

It did spread, seemingly overnight, and here is where I blacked out. Doesn't it seem like we went from intelligent programming featuring people with class to completely mindboggling, inane shows where we celebrate every creep, cretin, and lowlife we can find? And the worse you are, the better production value you have. Here are just a few of my favorite shows.

The Best of the TV Coma Shows

To Catch a Predator

Here was a show that gave us a look at the lowlifes that prey on young girls and boys. We saw all kinds of people, from doctors to plumbers, trying to get into the pants of small children. The first time, I have to admit, I watched it like everyone else. But then it became a reality show.

It was no longer a documentary, but a reality show making money and selling advertising space like any other show. Christ, can it get any more callous than that? I'm surprised they haven't come out with a *Ten Most Bodacious Pedophiles* show that we can all laugh along with. My personal favorite is the guy that brings his son along. I can see the DVD sales now: *Best of the Pedophiles: Volume 1.*

You know, this idea of a pedophile hiding behind every bush really has changed the world. I remember when I was growing up, my nieces and nephews would come to visit, and I would toss the young ones in the air and take them to the movies; never gave it a second thought. Well, no more. I won't allow anyone to leave me alone with their kid. Wouldn't do it. The world has become much too mad. It's sad, but there it is.

Maury Povich Show

When I watch this show, I feel like the cartoon characters whose eyes bug out of their heads. Can there be anything worse than realizing that the world is full of women trying to find out who of the four or five men they slept with is the father of their child? And we make it a show. It's on TV, people are watching it…AAARRRRH!

My Son is Not Immune to Reality

When you watch a reality show, do you believe that people really behave like that in real life? Do we throw food at each other like the Three Stooges, whom I personally consider well-mannered compared to some of the reality TV stars we have today? Do we shove everyone around and yell and scream? Do we swear like sailors? Are we so shallow that we can make even Paris Hilton wince? (Call me if this is your daily life.)

I caught my son watching this reality show where these young guys sell real estate in California. Don't get me wrong—they are quite successful, but they have cornered the market on shallowness. These guys have swum in the shallow pool all of their lives.

My son is watching an episode where one of the real estate guys is trying to get the manager of a new Hollywood high-rise to get him an exclusive listing for one of the penthouses. He gives her his pitch, and even throws in a little dog for good measure.

But I look at it and I think to myself, Are we all insane here? Has the world gone completely mad? Okay, they are sitting there, talking, but there are cameras everywhere, filming everything and you gotta believe that the woman managing the project sees the cameras. Isn't that a good assumption, or am I missing something? Can't she just go home and see past episodes of this show?

Hmmm, I think. I bet she's thinking, I give this guy a listing and my project is on TV forever. Let's see. Does that make sense? Do I need a great salesman for that? Of course she is going to give him the listing. She is not a nitwit.

My brain is beginning to hurt. I turn to my very intelligent son with an "I don't get it" look.

My son says, "It's a reality show."

I look at him suddenly like he isn't my son anymore but some pod person. But it's not any *real* reality.

"It's just entertainment," my son says. Oh God, I am going nuts.

To me, reality shows that pretend to be real, even though everyone is surrounded by cameras and there are makeup and hair people in the wings, is kind of like eating a wad of wasabi and having your brain feel permanently numb.

Crime Shows

I now realize that the producers of all *True Crime* shows either believe or know that we are all totally senile. Every couple of months, they announce a new *True Crime* show with brand-spanking-new episodes. Now, I like a good old husband-kills-wife or wife-kills-husband kind of show like anyone else, so I tune in.

About halfway through the new episode, I say, "What the hey? I've seen this before." All they've done is change the people they interview or pretend it's the dead person talking, but it's the same old lame husband-offs-wife or wife-offs-husband that you've seen many, many times before, just repackaged.

But maybe the TV producers are in the right; it still takes me half the show to realize that I've seen it before. Maybe next year I will forget and watch it again, and think it is new.

One of my favorite crime shows was with this guy who created a "scale of evil." Sounds so scientific, doesn't it? He pretends it is, with all its fancy labels for killers. He categorizes people on his scale with things like *maniac killer who liked his mom,* which is slightly better than just *maniac killer,* or worse, *maniac killer with no feelings of remorse.* What was really cool about this guy was that at the beginning of the show, he'd be seen typing on an Underwood typewriter. Where did he get such a thing, and why? He also would review things on a microfiche reader. Does anyone remember those things? Do libraries even have them anymore? I think someone should start asking questions about this guy.

Another one I really like is *Snapped.* The premise is women who kill men, but nine times out of ten, what that means is wives who kill their husbands; I think I caught my wife taking notes.

I think women should be given equal treatment when it comes to murders. Believe it or not, they always give the same lame excuses that men do. One of my all-time favorites was a woman who was so seriously sick of her husband that she killed him and left him in the bedroom. She then put up one of those threshold stops that keeps out drafts to block the smell. You know, those cloth things they make that look like snakes and you prop against the door to keep the cold out—only in her case, it was the smell. She had also lit a bunch of scented candles.

But what was really great was that she had a new boyfriend who apparently didn't smell anything, nor was he curious about the locked bedroom door. Wow, men are total maroons sometimes when it comes to babes and sex. They will do about anything for the latter; even pretend they don't smell Daryl in the other room.

DARE Coma

The DARE coma occurred on June 21, 2011 at my grandson's school. I was invited to see the DARE graduation, my grandson being one of the graduates. I am not making this up—I really had no idea what this was.

My wife and I drove to the school and headed toward the auditorium. As we entered, we were handed a playbill of the proceedings. I saw the word "DARE." And there it was. Coma over.

The program said DARE, which was an acronym for "Drug Abuse Resistance Education." What? My grandson was ten years old, for Christ's sake. I didn't know about three-two beer until junior high. God, to this day, I don't even know what three-two beer means. But here I am at a DARE graduation. Where did we go so wrong? How could this happen? Ten-year-old kids? Are we mad?

The kids with the best essays got up and read them. It was all stuff about making good choices about drugs and alcohol. What? This couldn't be happening. My grandson, the best person in the whole world, was actively making choices not to do drugs and alcohol. This couldn't be.

After the ceremony, I cornered my grandson about the whole thing. He informed me that 10 percent of all eighth graders drink. What? When did this happen? How did this happen? Was there a way to blame lawyers for this? There must be.

This wouldn't have happened in a world where there was any type of logic. This would never have happened in my parents' world, much less when my kids were growing up. What happened to us? How did we get to the point where the school has to enroll kids in this DARE program at age ten? It is complete madness.

I'm picturing TV ads in the future with a baby smoking a cig and drinking a scotch and soda and saying gaa gas goo goo with a subtitle saying, "Don't let this happen to your children". I'm trying to think how to blame the legal profession for the alcohol and drug problem but it escapes me at the moment.

There is a sign near my grandson's school that says, "drug-free school zone." Lately, I've begun wondering about the deeper meaning of the sign. Does this sign really stop the evildoers of the world, like some invisible shield? When a drug dealer wanders into the area, is there some voice that says, "Begone, you blaggard. This is a drug-free zone. You shall not pass into this school zone"? I'm picturing knights in armor guarding the school gates from the effluvium that might attempt to sell their drugs.

On the other hand, I have to wonder: if this is a drug-free school zone, is there a mandatory-drug zone? I would think there would have to be, given the state of our world and lawyers that inhabit this planet. We must have balance in all things, so we must have a drug zone, as it would probably be unconstitutional not to.

Odd Thoughts
TV Stuff

TV Ratings

I assume T.V. rating folks determine whether a show is a hit or not by either calling people to find out what they're watching, or monitoring what you are watching via some gizmo you have agreed to attach to the tube.

I have this image of someone calling me and asking me what I was watching, to which I would say, "I'm watching *Little Miss Perfect*. I never miss it." Would anyone really own up to such a thing? Or, "I am watching the continuing episodes of the reality folks pulling each other's hair and swearing a blue streak."

Does anyone really say they are watching *Masterpiece Theatre* or a special airing of the Shakespeare play *Henry IV?* Nope. Everyone is watching *Real Housewives of Orange County*. Makes you want to cry.

Infomercials

You know what I like to do? When I see an infomercial at 4 a.m. and the pitchman tells me that I only have ten minutes to get the extra-special deal, I will wait maybe twenty minutes before I call to make my purchase and insist on getting the extra-special deal. You know it always works. They aren't going to give me a hard time over missing the deadline by ten minutes or so.

Also, if they say there's a limit of ten doodad's per household, I always insist on having eleven. You can't put one over on me. I wasn't born yesterday.

Is there a school for infomercial actors? I'd love to attend one. I just can't get enough of those facial expressions they make when someone is hocking a product, like stuff for joint pain, and they have some person lean over, grab their back, and wince in pain.

Or if they're selling something that will enable you to reach higher, there's that look of frustration on the person's face as they are trying to reach something, before they get hold of a spiffy new extra arm-reacher. How about the knowing glances they give to each other when they realize that the product they just bought has made their lives one step away from nirvana?

I picture this school as having different departments so you can specialize in wincing with pain, or take classes in how to nod knowingly or shake your head in utter disbelief.

How do they pick the people for these commercials? Like the woman that does the Dulcolax commercials: does she just look like someone who is constipated at the beginning of the ad, then looks like she is unconstipated at the end? What talent. Is there a method acting school for this line of work? I think I could do constipated.

There are other great actors that should also get credit. There are those who do a phenomenal job of looking bloated or having blocked sinuses, or looking so depressed they can hardly move. Are there kids that grow up saying, "I want to be a TV commercial actor?" I don't remember the guidance counselor suggesting those things to me. Of course, my guidance counselor felt I should be working in a tile factory, or maybe meatpacking.

How do you get selected to do the testimonials for those lame products on TV anyway? I can slobber over stuff with the best of them. I can nod my head in the audience when the pitchman says, "Has this ever happened to you?" I have a laugh just as fake as anyone else's. How do people get those jobs?

I want to sit in an audience and nod my head knowingly, or look slightly perplexed over how this new gizmo does what it does so well until I'm told all the gory details, at which time I smile and nod my head some more. I can do it—just give me a chance, that's all I ask.

And ever notice how much TV commercials are like reality TV? "Welcome to Hidden Valley, where the kids love vegetables!" You see these kids with maniacal smiles munching on broccoli that's drenched in ranch dressing. Yeah right. My kids used to count the peas on their plates and question the fairness of why one of them had five while the other had six.

I want to be the guy who assigns a price to all the stuff you see on the tube. I'd sit at a desk with a jeweler's loupe and people would bring me their stuff. I'd look it over very carefully with my lens, ask questions about what it is and what it does, then inevitably stamp *$19.95* on the form.

Now, the person selling their stuff would say, "Hey, this is worth forty dollars," to which I'd say, "Sure it is, and we will certainly mention that in the ad, then add the amount to the shipping and handling." Everything is $19.95; doesn't really matter what it is.

Personally, I believe in every ad and what they are selling and what each thing is worth with my whole heart, even though each product is only an astounding $19.95.

I even have my own ideas for some products. So the other day, I'm brushing my teeth with an electric toothbrush, which I believe 110 percent of the population has, though you wonder why your dentist always hands you a spanking-new toothbrush that you end up putting in a drawer in case you have a thousand relatives show up with no toothbrushes. I digress.

So I'm brushing my teeth and I'm looking in the mirror when my wife appears, shaking her head and pointing at the toothbrush splatters on the mirror. So I slap my head with my hand in disgust while my wife hands me a paper towel and some Windex (with that "You created this mess, you clean it up" look.)

TV Stuff

Happen to you? Of course it does, but if you are like me, you wait a week or so before dragging out the Windex. My new $19.95 invention is this thing that fits around your neck and sticks out with a throwaway paper filter in front of your mouth (extra refills available to order, of course). Now you can brush your teeth without getting anything on the mirror, your wife smiles at the result, and the world is a better place.

Animal Stories

Squirrels

When I lived on Kenyon Street in Hartford, Connecticut, we had the occasional squirrel that would somehow get inside our house and run around in the walls. Not a good time to read *The Exorcist* with scratching in your ceiling.

Anyway, I tried everything: chicken wire, mothballs, group counseling with the squirrels. Then one day, I was walking down a dark alley somewhere when I heard a, *"Psst, psst."*

I was about to turn around, but the guy says, "Don't turn around. Keep walking straight. Don't look back."

I was terrified, but I kept moving forward.

He says, "I heard that you're having problems with squirrels. Don't answer—just keep walking and nod your head."

I nodded my head.

He then said, "Butcher's blood. Smear it on the place where they're getting in."

I looked back, but he was gone. Butcher's blood? Okay, I'll try anything.

So I go to Santilli's in Hartford. Mr. Santilli and I are buds 'cause I only get my steaks, chops, and everything else from him. He not only owns the joint, but he is also the butcher.

So I go in and he says, "What sounds good today?"

I say, "Anthony, I know this is going to sound completely nuts, but I need butcher's blood."

He doesn't eye me like someone that needs a straightjacket. He says, "Squirrel trouble?"

I nod my head, and he walks off and comes back with a plastic container, like you see used for parmesan cheese, filled with what is butcher's blood, I guess. I thanked him and head home.

On the way home, I start thinking, what the heck is butcher's blood? Did Anthony go in the back room and slit his wrist for me? Not likely. Must be some magic combination of different animals' blood. So I go home and dutifully smear the stuff over the opening where the squirrels are getting in. I kind of feel like this is some kind of squirrel voodoo rite I'm performing.

Meanwhile, my neighbor, John Bermon uses the Havahart trap method. He traps them and then drops them off somewhere else. I told him he was wasting his time. Squirrels are one of the smartest creatures on this earth; I told him that if he painted a number on the next squirrel he trapped, he would see that same squirrel a week later.

I started imagining a squirrel taxi that picks up the Havahart trap guys, driven by some squirrel guy named Phil:

Phil:

Hey, Jerry how goes the battle?

Jerry:

Been pretty well, Phil. Got trapped, but the food in the trap was pretty good. Actually, Phil, can you step on it? Jane and the kids are waiting. But hey, Phil, you'll get a kick out of this-the Hansons used butcher's blood to keep us out. Stuff tastes pretty good.

Phil:

(snickering) That's rich.

But I do contend that squirrels are incredibly smart. They have the patience of Job when it comes to defeating you with your bird feeder. They will try and try and try until they figure it out.

Plastic? Hah! Child's play. They merely eat through it. Wood? Double-hah!

When my mother sent me the ultimate bird feeder, I thought, there is no way the squirrels will ever figure this one out. It is metal with a slanting lid that is very slippery. There is a platform for the birds, but with the slightest weight, the platform moves down and closes off the food.

I watched the squirrels try and try and try and try. They would jump on the top, and then try their best to hang on to the roof with one toenail while they reached over to get the seeds. Sorry, squirrels—they always fell off.

They would try everything. They would jump on the top to try to dislodge it. They would push at the pole holding it up, but with no success. This went on for years, and I knew my mother had sent me the final "squirrel-proof" bird feeder. But no, my friend. Oh no.

One day, I'm looking out the window and I see something in the bird feeder—and it's no bird.

It was successfully hanging there, eating the seeds without tripping the platform. I was amazed. It had been at least ten years, but some squirrel had moved on in the evolutionary scale of squirrels, so I went out to figure out how it was done. What the squirrel had figured out was that there was a half-inch gap on the inside of the feeder where the lid fit down over the feeder. The squirrel had figured out that if they got in the feeder while they were turned upside down, then put their toes through the gap, they could hang there and eat the seeds.

I'll tell you this. If squirrels ever figure out how to cross the street, they will be running for senate.

Flies

Where do flies go when they aren't bugging you? You put the food away, and the flies are gone. Bring the food back outside, and boom, there they are again. Do flies have homes? What do they look like? Do flies have scouts with binoculars looking for someone having a picnic?

"Hey, Bob, picnic at ten o'clock."

"Locked in, Jim. Preparing to land on potato salad."

"Jim, pull up, pull up, for God's sake! Flyswatter at noon!"

Where do they go in the winter? Do they pack up and go to Florida where I am? If so, they really do keep to themselves down here, though it could be the constant bug spray that does them in.

Do flies constantly hover around your door waiting for you to leave it open so they can drop in (without even a "by your leave," I might add)? And once they get in, why are they so interested in finding a way out again, buzzing around the window like it is just magically going to open? And if you decide to have a heart and just open the window, they climb higher, like they really just want to be annoying rather than leave. Am I imparting too much brainpower on a fly?

Since there is so much fast food today for flies to feast on, are there obese flies now? Do they join fly weight watchers? Maybe, they switch to Nutrisystem meals. Just asking.

Mosquitos

I know we've all thought about how odd these things are. I mean, they subsist on drinking the blood of others.

Which came first? The mosquito or some animal with some blood they could suck. If the former, what were they eating before we came along? Was there once an herbivorous mosquito? I'm told that only the females go for the blood. Do they bring it home to hubby? I can just hear it now: "Not O-positive again! What about some AB once in a while?"—"Hey, buster, why don't you learn how to suck blood and get your own?"

Given the way we eat today and the fat problem, do mosquitoes get checked by mosquito doctors for high cholesterol? Do they take statins? Inquiring minds want to know.

And why does it have to itch after they bite you? Is this some kind of punishment for a sin committed a million years ago? I mean, they can have a little blood if they want, but I don't know why they have to inject that itchy stuff. I guess it's their way of saying, "Gotcha." Or perhaps if you didn't itch you would look around and there would be a 20 pound mosquito on your arm and you would be out a pint of blood.

There are millions of sprays and noisemaking gadgets that supposedly gets rid of the little beasts, but you can't keep a good mosquito down. But I have a solution: my wife. She is an absolute mosquito magnet. If she is standing anywhere within a mile radius of a single mosquito, they will come. I'd like to hire her out for parties; just send her out to the backyard, and bam, no one else gets bitten.

I, on the other hand, am the complete reverse. No self-respecting mosquito would bite me unless there was nothing left on the planet. I'm not sure why my blood is not to their liking. However, there have been times when they must have been desperate and I've gotten a mosquito bite. When this happens, I tell people to head for the hills if you value your life and sanity.

Household Items

Grout

Why is there tile grout? And even worse, why is it white 99 percent of the time? I think it was invented by the person who invented all of the stuff that supposedly cleans it up, which never actually works.

Have you tried every product known to man to get your tiles white again? I have: vinegar, Tilex, Soft Scrub. You name it and I've tried it, with zero success. To me, white grout is for people who have learned how to levitate over their floors so that they never touch it.

And why is white grout always used in the rooms that are most likely to get dirty? It's always in the kitchen and bathroom. I don't know about you, but I've spilled my share of whatever in the kitchen and the grout seems to just suck it up and laugh at me. And what about bathroom showers? Are you kidding? Those are some of the scummiest places on the planet.

They now have these new sprays that you can use every time you take a shower. I haven't seen any difference in the bathroom shower, but I'm a shade lighter.

Angie's List

I think the time has come to use Angie's list for other things besides home repair. It really should be expanded to include politicians to take all the guesswork out of picking your next representative. You'd just look at the reviews and make a selection.

And how about ladies of the evening? You could get an honest review from your neighbors. Take all the guess work out of sex. How about hired killers? You get an unbiased review of how well they did the job, costs, and keeping their mouths shut. In today's world the latter being the most important.

What about drug dealers? Who gives you the best weed for your money without opening fire on you?

Best arsonists, kidnappers…oh never mind

Detergent

My detergent says it will do 120 loads, but has anyone ever verified this? What if it doesn't? Can you take it back for a refund? Do they have a guy who tests the number of loads? That's his job; he comes in every morning and washes loads of laundry to find out how many loads can be done with one bottle. Does he have regular staff meetings to discuss the results, assuming there's one guy for Tide and another for Cheer?

I think most of the detergent in the world is made by Proctor and Gamble. I picture the conveyor belt with empty bottles of All, Tide, and Wisk, and that the same liquid pours into each bottle. I mean, it all looks the same, doesn't it?

Garage, Tag, and Yard Sales

The time has come, my friends, to establish a legal definition of BIG, GIGANTIC, HUGE, LARGE, and MEGA as they pertain to tag sales. My wife and I are sick and tired of waking up on a Saturday or Sunday and shaking off the cobwebs with a cup of Joe so we can make it early to a *huge* or *gigantic* or even *mega* tag sale, only to find out it is a couple of dilapidated card tables with the same salad spinner, moldy old candles, or the remains of some crafted thing that went bad that we have all seen before. I am sick and tired of it.

There ought to be a law, damn it. There's no standard definition. Anybody can submit an ad to the local paper that says "MEGA garage sale," and the person taking the ad never says, "Sir, are you sure this is MEGA and not just BIG?" There has got to be a real definition of what these terms mean.

Why should I get out of bed for teeny-weenie garage sale? When you say MEGA, it should have some meaning. I suggest that each state hire a bunch of people at the taxpayers' expense to go to the MEGA or HUGE, or GIGANTIC site and make an assessment before we poor suckers end up spending out time and gas on these bogus sales.

I also think that certain items that should be banished from yard sales. I think we have seen enough unused exercise bikes and other gym equipment that is draped with used laundry before it hits the washing machine. And what about aperitif glasses? Does anyone really use these things anymore? No. A resounding *no*. Throw them at your fireplace and make a wish, but don't try fobbing them off on us anymore. And rusty old tools; what the do I need with another rusty screwdriver or saw with the teeth missing?

And how about estate sales? Estate sales used to mean that the person was dead, so now all of their junk was on display whether they liked it or not. Estate sales say, "You have to pay more because the people are dead and can't withhold the good stuff. You have the ability to buy anything they owned. They have no say because they are dead" But no more, my friend. I attended an estate sale where the people were very much alive, but felt their junk was higher-grade junk and thus fit the criteria of "estate" sale.

To this I say, "No, no, *no*." You have to be dead or at least on life support in order to have an estate sale.

12-Item Aisle

I would like the government to stop wasting time on stuff like stimulus and unemployment and concentrate on the real issues of the day. One of the ones that I think really needs to be clarified is the twelve-items-or-less checkout line.

What does *twelve* really mean? If I buy some cat food, say three for a dollar, do the three cans count as one item? I always feel uneasy in line when I buy three cartons of Coke for some sale price. I leave two in the cart, but does that count? Are the people behind me adding it up in their heads and shaking their heads over what the world is coming to, thinking that there is no ethics, no scruples?

And here I am in line with eleven items, plus two extra Coke twelve-packs. I would really like some clarification.

When you are standing in the 12 or less aisle, have you ever pondered the lives of people based on the items they purchase? So you see someone in front of you with KY jelly and strawberries what comes to mind? Sometimes I see whipped cream, a hammock, and a mounds bar. I leave it to you to figure out.

Newspapers

I know a lot of folks are not bemoaning the end of print media. "Hey, I can read it on my PC, or my phone, or any handheld device."

But hold up there. Wait just a cotton pickin' minute. I think everyone should really sit back and consider the global implications of losing the print media. I am going to name just a few of the devastating effects it might have on the world:

Has anyone considered what would happen to the Silly Putty industry? To me, the most entertaining thing to do with Silly Putty is stamping it flat on a picture of *Hagar the Horrible* from the comic strips, then lifting it off and stretching it out to create hilarious images. Without the print media, then what? I can't imagine there would be much use for Silly Putty then, can you?

Really, the worst impact will be on first and second graders who will be unable to develop their artistic capabilities by making paper-Mache Easter bunnies and Halloween pumpkins. I shudder to think what is going to happen then; think about a world where there are no more paper-Mache things. Think of the impact on Mexico and the piñata. And without the piñata, there really isn't any need to make all of that stale candy that goes inside, or the sticks to whack the piñata, or the handkerchiefs used to blindfold the kids. Whole industries will be destroyed.

On a totally selfish level, I wonder how I'll be able to paint anymore. I'm not like those people on those *Sell My House* shows who can paint a whole carpeted room while dressed in their finest duds and not get paint all over everything. I need newspaper in vast quantities all over everything before I start to paint, and I gotta believe there are lots of folks who are going to be in the same boat. Are we going to have to go to Home Depot to buy fake newspaper? Will it look like the old newspaper, or will it have fake Home Depot ads?

What about fireplaces? Have you ever considered how you're going to start a fire in the old fireplace without newspaper? Good luck. I know I know they have those starter sticks, but I challenge you to light them without newspaper. Goodbye, winter fires.

Think of the impact this is going to have on the mafia. Previously, if they had wanted to instill fear in their enemies, they would kill someone, wrap a fish in a newspaper, and then send it to their rivals with a note that says: "Guido now lies with the fishes."

Now what? It's not going to have the same impact if you wrap the fish in Reynolds wrap. Someone is just likely to poke some holes in the top and put it on the grill.

What about the impact on eBay? I don't know about you, but I don't have an endless supply of bubble wrap or those horrible Styrofoam peanuts lying around; I use newspaper to wrap that treasure or junk before I send to someone else. Am I going to have to go out and buy fake newspaper to do that in the future?

I don't know. Seems to me we should rethink this whole extinction of print media thing.

Candy

Does anyone really eat JuJu Bees? Or Circus Peanuts? Or Mexican Hats? I believe that the last box of Mexican Hats was made in October of 1959 in a little town in Mississippi, and that we have been working off the inventory ever since.

I've got to admit though, Pez dispensers are pretty cool. You have to love those little plastic heads of Darth Vader, or the Halloween pumpkins with the permanent tracheotomies, Pez popping out of their throats. But seriously, have you ever really eaten one of those things? Really, all the Pez folks have to do is make the dispensers; you can use the same packet of Pez forever.

I saw this catalog once where this company was going to bring back some old-time favorites for us to enjoy. One was Blackjack Gum. I had to laugh. I know most of you folks out there don't remember, but if I remember correctly, that wrapper was black on blue, and what was inside was truly awful. Black licorice gum. Yum doesn't get any better that that. I shook my head at the time, thinking, Wow, that's bound to be a big seller.

What about Neco Wafers? Did anyone really eat those? We used to line them up and shoot at them with a BB gun. And what about Bit O' Honey? We used to dread getting this stuff handed to us on Halloween. We would look at each other, nod our heads, and say, "Be back with the soap later."

The one I did miss, or thought I did, was the Bun Bar. It was this white stuff covered with chocolate and peanuts that I ate as a kid. Thirty years later, my sister and I were waiting for our mother at the hospital. We are both grown and should have known better, but we saw Bun Bars in the candy machine.

We both said, "Wow!", slapped our money in and each got one. There was no sharing the old Bun Bar.

We both took a bite, looked at each other, and spit them out laughing hysterically. Either they were a lot better way back when, or our tastes had dramatically changed.

Easter Candy

I kind of lost track of chocolate bunnies until my grandson was born, and I have to say, it is a sad, sad situation. Sure, you can still get the Easter Peeps with the one eye on the side of their heads (thank God for some traditions), but chocolate bunnies? Man. When I was growing up, we must have been spoiled rotten.

First of all, none of us would have anything to do with hollow bunnies. Don't bother, folks, we weren't going to eat it. They had to be solid chocolate, and not only solid chocolate, but fully three-dimensional and at least eight inches high as well.

Today? You're kidding me. First of all, I've notice most of the chocolate says "chocolate-flavored." What does that mean? Are these wax bunnies coated with something that is chocolate-flavored as opposed to real chocolate? And who even makes chocolate flavoring? I see it as a byproduct of some laundry detergent made at Procter and Gamble, something left over after making Wisk.

To me, the only one who makes decent-tasting chocolate bunnies is Russell Stover, but even theirs are only two-dimensional. Okay, they have three dimensions, but the thickness of those babies can't be any more than a quarter-inch. As I said, it's a sad, sad world we live in.

What happens to all that Easter candy after Easter? Where do all the bunnies go? Do we distribute them to the poor in the inner cities? Do we melt them down to create Milky Way bars? I mean, one day the market is full of Easter candy, and the next day it's all gone. Is there an Easter candy graveyard somewhere filled with the bodies of bunnies and chickies? Or is there some parallel, Easter-themed universe they all go to? Has anyone interviewed a supermarket employee on this matter, or are they sworn to secrecy?

Or have you ever contemplated marshmallow Peeps? Those blobs of marshmallow colored yellow or pink or purple, with the vaguest outline of a beak and one eye on the side of their heads? Have you ever wondered who designed the Peep?

I am praying it was some abstract artist, otherwise I very much fear that there was a nuclear meltdown somewhere that we don't know about.

Life Alert

You gotta shake your head over the way he died, naked in a hotel closet with a rope around his neck and balls. I find it hard to picture. But wouldn't you say old Dave is a poster boy for Life Alert? I mean, if he had it, he could have pushed the button and heard, "Hello, Mr. Carradine, are you in need of assistance?"

Then he could have just said, "I'm naked in a closet and strangling, and I can't seem to get out." He'd be alive today.

Repairs

So you call to get an appliance fixed, one that you have a warranty for, and the person at the other end of the call says, "I can schedule that for next Monday between the hours of 8 and 5." Wow, doesn't get any better than that. Now I can sit around from 8 to 5 staring at my broken appliance, not that I have a choice, seeing as they aren't giving me any.

But did you ever wonder who the 8 a.m. person is? Has it ever been you? I think not. You and I are the 4:30, or better yet, you get the call from the repairman saying, "I'm running late. I'll be there at 5:30."

Or the repairman says, "I'm stuck at another customer we will have to reschedule for tomorrow." Of course when you ask what time they are coming you get, "Between 8 and 5".

So who ends up getting the 8 a.m.? How do they rate? Are they related to the Fix-It guy? Did they pay more for their warranty than I did to get that extra-special service? No, I actually think there is only one appointment per day at 5:00 p.m. The rest of the day, the Fix-It guy is doing his banking, or getting groceries, or playing cards, or whatever.

So they finally come to your house. Now, you desperately want this guy to have the part to fix your appliance, but you know in your heart that they won't. They didn't even ask you what brand of appliance you have and even if they had, I don't suppose you could expect them to have every part available.

So they come and they hem and they haw, and then say, "Yep, it's broken. It needs a new frazzlelator, which I have to order. Should be in a week or so. When we get it, we'll schedule another appointment." (He means between the hours of 8 and 5 AAAAARRRRGH!!

But I feel even sorrier for the poor slob who doesn't have a warranty. The Fix-It guy comes and says, "Yes, your appliance is broken and you need a new frazzlelator, but it just so happens that the new frazzlelator will cost more than your appliance. That will be $69, please."

Car Trouble

My Rav 4

I have a Toyota Rav 4. It has a tachometer. For those in the know, a tachometer measures your wheels' revolutions per minute. When I was sixteen, if you didn't have a car with a tachometer, you were a total loser. I remember driving my folks' Pontiac Bonneville with no tachometer and being totally humiliated.

Funny thing is, I don't know what those things are used for or why they are even cool. I mean, do you know something interesting by knowing the number of revolutions your wheels make? Do people say, "Shoot, my car's only doing 2000 revolutions." I never understood it, but I'm glad my Rav 4 has one.

Anyway, when I was seventeen, my father bought me a 1963 Ford Falcon; it was bright red, or maybe orange. It had the magic tachometer, and my father changed out the engine for the biggest Ford engine the car would take. I think it was a 252 or 257—forgive me if I get it wrong.

This one time, I came up to a traffic light and a GTO was beside me. The GTO owner revs his engine, looks over at me, and smiles. It's one of those deprecating smiles, one of those smiles where if you were bigger and stronger, you'd get out of your 1963 Falcon and wipe it off his face, but you don't 'cause you're me. But the situation is so cool. After all, you gotta believe there is no

Car Trouble

contest between a GTO and a lowly 1963 Ford Falcon. That is a Ford Falcon that has not been modified by your father

The light turns green, and I'm in the next county before the GTO gets two feet. I loved my dad very much.

My current Rav 4 has a speedometer that goes up to 140 miles per hour. Now, raise your hand if your VW Bug or Ford Echo can go to 140 mph. Do you suppose a normal car can actually go that fast? Do car manufacturers really test the ability of a car to reach 140 mph? I gotta wonder where going 140 would come in handy? I live in Florida and I have crossed Alligator Alley; I suppose you could try to go 140 mph, but my wife might question the wisdom of this. Plus, I gotta believe the car is going to start groaning at that kind of speed.

So what does it all mean? I guess if you are in the passing lane and the guy beside you is doing 130 mph, you need the ability to do 140 mph to get past him. Or maybe the 140 is so you can outrun a police officer, if you think that's a great idea. Which reminds me...

I live in Naples, Florida, average speed 45 mph. However, beware the street of Shadowlawn. The speed limit there is 25 mph, with a reduction to 20 mph in the school zone—very handy when the police department needs some ready cash.

My wife and I were travelling down Shadownlawn at the unheard of speed of 35 mph when I got pulled over. The officer takes my license and registration, and then goes back to his car to make sure I haven't recently robbed a bank. (Don't tell me you don't break out in the same sweat. You know you didn't do anything, but maybe there is a cloned you out there somewhere doing evil things.)

Anyways, the police officer comes back and says, "Mr. Hanson, did you realize you were doing 35 miles an hour in a school zone?"

"But Mr. Officer," I say. "It's July 1st and school is out."

"That doesn't matter, Mr. Hanson."

The result? $200 fine.

But in Florida, there is hope for the evildoers. You can go to evildoers' school to reduce your fine and not get any points.

So I went and signed up for Florida's evildoers' school. Now, the way it works is that you go to the school to learn the evil of your ways so that you can expunge that evil 35-miles-per-hour ticket.

I went in and took my seat. There are TV cameras hanging from the ceiling, and Diane Sawyer is talking about driving, asking questions and giving answers. I think, Christ on a crutch (as my sainted ma used to say), I should be writing this stuff down. There's going to be a quiz after we are done.

I listen for about an hour, taking notes, before the teacher shows up. It is then that I am totally enlightened. I discover that most of the folks in the room either speak Spanish or Haitian. I now realize that this is not a note-taking situation. This is just a Florida sit-here, collect-the-fee, stamp-a-form, go-home situation. But there is one, and only one, catch.

The teacher, if that's what you want to call him says, "People, there is only one rule. You get one break. The break is for fifteen minutes. You must be back in fifteen minutes. If you don't return within the fifteen minutes, the door will be locked and you will lose your stamped 'I came to traffic school' form."

Later on, we get the fifteen minute break, and everyone, including me, runs outside. Most folks want a smoke. As a former smoker, I can totally relate.

So we're milling around like we're the inmates in some penitentiary. Picture it: we're all outside in the "yard," talking about our crimes. One guy said he was going 140 mph in his Rav 4 on Alligator Alley. Another said this was the tenth time they had been picked up for speeding. Another guy attempted to outrun the police. Then they all focused on me. What had I done to do the time?

I told them I had been doing 35 in a 20 mph zone.

Cold stares. I was scared for my life.

But here's what is totally unbelievable: after the fifteen minutes, we all marched back in and sat down, and as promised, the door was locked. After ten minutes, there were people banging on the door. They couldn't get back within the fifteen minute limit. They pleaded and cajoled in English, Spanish, and Haitian. The teacher was having none of it.

My Rav 4 has an automatic transmission, but it does have an L, 2, and 3, as well as the usual D, R, and N. I have the D, R, and N pretty well figured out, but the L, 2, and 3 have me baffled. It's like when you see some ancient rite that goes on and on and makes absolutely no sense today, but people keep doing it. For example, throwing salt over your shoulder apparently has something to do with Judas spilling salt at the last supper. Kind of silly but we keep doing it. So the car has these settings that I don't think anyone uses any more unless they are trying to scale Mt Everest with their Rav4 and need L 2 and 3 to make it to the summit. I picture a Sherpa saying, "Mr. Hanson, you simply will have to put the RAV4 in L if you want to make it to the top".

My Rav 4 tells me how fast I'm going in kilometers, if you care to know. When I was growing up, I had teachers who told us the metric system was coming, that it was just a matter of time. We were all going to convert to metric eventually, like it or not. Instead of good old miles, we would have kilometers. "Weigh me out some kilograms, if you please."—"I think it is 200 meters to the green."

I know, I know. Our own system of measurement is really bizarre. There's one inch, and then twelve inches in a foot, then three feet in a yard, but you can get your head around all of it, can't you? True, the metric system really is much simpler, based on the tens of things involved, but give me 5,280 feet in a mile anytime, or an elephant that weighs ten tons—that means something to me.

If you say an elephant weights ten kilograms or whatever, well, it really sounds kind of effeminate to me. An elephant should be in tons—*tons* sounds masculine, *tons* is solid; *kilograms* is very wimpy.

You know the one place where metrics make sense? When you are weighing yourself, 'cause you won't know exactly what it means. "Am I an obese, fat slob, or am I losing weight?" Doesn't matter.

By the way, just in case you wanted to know, if you drive your Rav 4 140 mph, you are going 220 kilometers per hour, which, I gotta admit, sounds very impressive.

Pintos

Remember the Pinto automobile? Come on, it hasn't been totally wiped out of the collective unconscious, has it? I owned two of those beauties. But I realized all of a sudden, or *suddenly* as my English teacher would say, that they were no more. I mean, it's like they were literally swallowed up in some cosmic vortex. I've even seen Gremlins on commercials. Isn't there one Pinto out there somewhere? Where did they all go?

I think the government should give me some money to investigate. It might be of the utmost importance. What if the Terminator discovered that in some time in the future, robots will require some part from the Pinto, and so they all came from the future and took them all, but no one noticed?

I'd say that would be pretty important.

Gasoline

Why do all gas prices end in 9? I mean, it's not like you're buying a bedroom set that's $999.99 so you can say, "Wow what a deal." Last time I looked, you have very little choice when buying gas. I mean, when you see gas at $3.53 and 9/1000s instead of $3.54 do you say, "Wow! What a deal I'm gonna run right down and get me some of that $3.53 and 9/1000s gas while the gettin's good". Just asking. Inquiring minds want to know.

Getting Some Air

Remember going to a gas station to get air for your tires? Every gas station had this thing that looked like a small parking meter painted red. It had a crank on the side, and you used this crank to decide how much air you needed. Then you'd take the hose, connect it to your tire, and the thing would go *gajink, gajink* until you filled the tire to the pressure you had selected with the crank. Couldn't be any simpler.

Car Trouble

Today? Forget it. First, I don't think anyone's tires go flat anymore 'cause most gas stations don't even offer air. And if they do, you've got to feed it quarters to even get it going. Then you have to connect it to your tire, hold down the lever, and then release it to see this brass-colored gauge pop out and attempt to read the pressure.

You've got to be kidding me. Somebody bring back that red parking meter.

Finding Your Car

I want a gizmo that calls you when you leave a store and says, "Pssst, hey, Bill. Your car is over here." I know, I know, you are all saying, "Hey, just remember where your car is in the first place."

Sure, easy for you to say, but when I come to a store and the lot is empty, I think, "Piece of cake, I can find my car." Problem is, you go in one side of the store and come out on the other, and suddenly, the whole parking lot has filled up while you were inside.

Is it a macho thing not to pay attention to where your car is, or does it transcend gender? Someone should do a study. Personally, I think the Shadow (Lamont Cranston) is still alive and clouds men's minds when they park so that they can't remember where the hell their cars are.

Childproof and Childish

Childproof

I want to have a legal form created that says, "I am an adult. I want my pill bottles to open with a simple flip of my thumb. I promise I will not give my children these pills to open." I have not found a teenager yet who is interested in downing a bottle of statins. Well, no normal teenage that is.

I want my butane lighter to have a clicker on it that is similar to any gun on the open market. Show me a gun that requires you to push a button on the top with one finger, use another finger to push down the slide on the side, and then pull the trigger to get a flame. The funny thing is that I have to ask my grandson to light a candle for me.

Speaking of butane lighters, how much butane is really in those things? To me it seems like they have about four clicks' worth of butane, then that's it. That's why they aren't see-through. The maker of the butane lighter doesn't want you to see there is only enough butane to light 3 candles. And why do they all have that dial on them that allows you to adjust the flame? I challenge anyone to get those lighters to work at anything but the highest setting.

I want to see an end to those little circles that have a picture of something with a line through it, and then underneath, a caption that says, "No." You see this kind of stuff everywhere you look. Don't stand your child on his head in the grocery store cart; don't bring live ammo into the store; no propane tanks, especially if you are smoking a cig; don't shave with paper shredders; don't attempt to pierce your tongue with them either. Do they really have to tell you not to smoke in a lung cancer ward? I am totally tired of it.

Of course we can all blame lawyers for all of this. Most companies would "hope" you aren't a complete imbecile, but the lawyers have decided that you are and should therefore be protected if you do something imbecilic.

I want to be able to ride my bike without a helmet without being made to feel guilty. Christ, you'd think there was a death every four seconds from not wearing a bike helmet. And consider this: I only ride on sidewalks, so I could only possibly have a head-on collision with a pedestrian. I promise I won't sue. But you know what? Most people probably would.

Being Mean

Have you ever been driving behind a truck that has an 800 number and the caption, "How's my driving?" Have you ever wanted to call that number and tell them, "Hey, that guy is a real jerk, weaving all over the road and stuff. He almost killed me! Sick."

Or consider America's Most Wanted: have you ever wanted to call in and turn in your neighbor as the current serial killer they are hunting? I've pictured it a million times; I'd call the hotline and say I am positive that the serial killer they are looking for is living right next door to me. God, it would be great to watch the cops pull up to your neighbor's door. I don't know why I think that would be funny.

I want to visit someone with Obsessive Compulsive Disorder, specifically someone that is constantly cleaning their house. While they are cleaning, I'd say, "Hey, bucko. I think you missed a spot."

I'd like to visit a hoarder, you know, one of those folks that fills their house with junk. I'd say, "Hey, Marge, I heard there's a big sale at Target today, and it looks to me like you could use a few things for the house."

Impressing People

I had my car keys lying around when a friend of mine noticed them and said, "I see you have a Beamer." I looked over at Mr. Sherlock Holmes, and then realized that I did indeed have a key on my keychain that identified me as a BMW owner. So I thought, Hmm.

Want to get a pretty girl? Get yourself a Ferrari key. Next time you're in a bar trying to pick up chicks, casually drop your keychain on the bar. Of course, "the car is in for repair," but you go get the girl and worry about that later. (How childish. But then again, I acknowledge that I am childish. That's why my grandson and I get along so well; he looks at me and treats me as an equal.)

Now for this one, you'll just have to imagine the result of your actions. Next time you are at the gym, before you get off the weight machine, set the weight at the highest level. Then the next time someone sits down and looks at the weight, they'll think, Geez, I must be a total weakling. I couldn't lift that much weight if my life depended on it.

Like I said, *childish* is my middle name.

Way Out There Thoughts

Moccasins

It wasn't until I moved to Florida that it occurred to me just why the American Indians didn't stand a chance against the hordes of Europeans that dropped themselves here. It wasn't better weapons or greater numbers, my friend: it was the moccasins.

When I retired to Florida, I found that one has to have a comfortable pair of moccasins. These are the dress shoes of south Florida. Every shop has them. Now, I am making the assumption that they were made by Indians. They are marketed that way, but in this day and age, I found you can say just about anything and make it sound like the truth. But I digress.

So, I have my spiffy moccasins and I wear them everywhere, but I have found that those leather laces are impossible to keep tied. Now again, I am assuming that these are authentic moccasins, just like the Indians of yore wore. Anyway, the laces always come untied, and I am constantly tripping over them.

So I started picturing Indians-versus-white men battles. The general would say, "Hey, Chief, your shoes are untied." The chief would look down, and that would be that.

Or the Indians would be running after the white men, and just as they get a bead on them, boom, they trip over their mocs.

The editor of my book feels I am being rather insensitive as it is unlikely the native American Indians were killed off because the shoe laces on their moccasins came untied. For the record, I am of the opinion that the American Indians were totally outnumbered by the European hoards who decided "might makes right" and as an aside probably do not make today's moccasins that come untied in the first place. I am sure they come from some province in China.

Collective Unconscious

I subscribe to the Jungian notion of a collective unconscious where we are all born with certain shared experiences. If it's true, wouldn't it be cool if you could alter them? Big corporations could make it so that when a baby is born, the kid instantly wants a Happy Meal or has a pressing need to check out the smiley face discounts at Walmart.

Hey, what happens when you're cloned? Does all that stuff go with it? I mean, will the cloned me remember me? Will he insist on being called Bill even though his parents named him Nathan?

Stopping Time

Every time I hear an explanation of Einstein's theory of relativity, they discuss how time would stand still you approached the speed of light and always have these mindboggling experiments to prove it.

You don't have to understand Einstein's theory of relativity to see time stand still just go try to have your car registered at the DMV, or sit in an examining room waiting for the Dr. to show up, or get behind me in any line at the supermarket (I always appear to pick the slooooooow line), or how about your local social security office. You could probably add some weeks to your life given how time stands still.

Someone Owes Me Some Time

I think someone owes me about five to ten years of life, but I am wondering where I go to get it.

So this is my thought process: when I was young, my dad would pull up the gas station where Mike Zifer would come out to fill the tank, check the oil and tire pressure, and shoot the breeze with my dad. Now, how long did all that take compared to inserting your credit card, pumping gas, and leaving? I'd say ten to fifteen minutes each time. I figure I'm due at least six months for this.

What about grocery stores where there were no barcodes? The checkout person used a manual register to add up all the stuff and weigh all the produce. Now, you can zip through the self-checkout. How much time did I save with this innovation? A month, at least.

Hey, what about GPS? Prior to that, someone had to unroll the maps and even stop along the roads to find out where the hell we are. I'm figuring that's a solid month there too.

Cellphones: when travelling before, you'd have to stop, find a phone booth, deposit the required amount of coins (or stop and get change if you didn't have any), and make the calls. What do you say? How much time did that cost me? Two months? Three?

What about finding out what is written on the Statue of Liberty? Go to the library, find a Funk & Wagnall's and look it up. Today, google it. That's a couple of weeks, I'm thinking.

So the way I see it, I deserve at least a couple of years of my life back. Can someone tell me where I go to collect?

Cool Thoughts

Wouldn't it be cool if you sat down in an old Thunderbird, turned on the radio, and all the stations were playing '50s music?

You know those old paperback books that have the order forms in the back listing books for 25 cents? Wouldn't be cool if you filled one out, sent it in, and got the books?

I went to Hawaii once and saw signs that said, "Please do not remove the lava." I thought about that, given that Hawaii is a vast lava island. Can you imagine the headlines? "Hawaii Disappears; Tourist Takes Last piece of Hawaiian Islands."

Einstein—I think it was Einstein—said that light could not be destroyed. When you look up in the sky at night you, see the light reflected off some star some gazillion miles away. In fact, for all you know, the star grew up, had children, and then went to the dark side.

So if the only reason you and I are seen is because of reflected light, what would happen if we went into some black hole, captured some light, and played back the images? You could see Jesus walking on water, or maybe Mrs. Guiner winning the weekly bingo game at her church.

One thing Einstein was wrong about was the speed of light. He theorized that you could not go faster than the speed of light. I am afraid he was totally mistaken. At some future time when your RAV4 can do the speed of light and you are going down Alligator Alley in Florida, someone will surely pass you on the left.

Bill's Personal Rants

Integrity

Remember integrity? No? Well, it was the idea that you stood for something that your word was binding. You did the right thing and stood by what you did. Those days are long gone, and we can thank lawyers for this to a large extent. Integrity? Who needs integrity? There's no money in integrity.

Remember when songwriters wouldn't let their material be used for commercial purposes? Now, wave a fifty in front of their faces and they would sell their songs to sell dog poop if they could make a buck off it.

Where has all the integrity gone? Long time passing. Look at any lawyer on the planet if you want to see a lack of integrity. Look at any Wall Street brokerage house if you want to see the face of lost integrity. Look at any mortgage banker who loaned money to people who couldn't afford it, all at the expense of the rest of us, to see lost integrity.

Look at Congress, who pushed and threatened the lending institutions into disastrous financial positions. Look at the people behind the financial rating systems like Moody's and Standard & Poor's who didn't have the guts to stand up and say, "Hey, this is totally wrong."

I just heard "Help" being played in an H.H. GREGG ad advertising appliances. We are certainly all going to hell.

Defining Tacky

There was a time when you could easily define *tacky*. You could look at something and say with confidence, "Yes, that is tacky" While growing up in Ohio, being a very sensitive young lad, I was tacky aware. I knew what tacky was. There was no gray area; tacky involved lawn ornaments. Specifically, chrome balls, pink flamingos, steel milk containers, planted plastic flowers, and black stable boys holding a lantern.

But the bar for tacky just keeps rising because now everything is tacky. TV is tacky, our Congressmen are tacky, reality stars are tacky. In fact, I must say even my own ability to judge tacky has been clouded. After moving to south Florida, I not only enjoy pink flamingos on my lanai, I prefer them to light up when I plug them in.

Today we are overwhelmed by tacky to such an extent that the old tacky is now blended with the new tacky, and it has become very difficult to put your finger on what exactly tacky is. Well, on second thought, I think everyone would agree that black stable boys with lanterns are still tacky.

We really need some kind of tacky-o-meter that has an arrow marked with some numbers that measure the inches (and centimeters for the European market) of tackiness. You raise the tacky-o-meter to something like a TV show, and it would register the levels of tacky present. I agree that the initial calibration would be a problem since the tacky bar keeps moving, but I think it could be done.

We can take it to the Maury Povich show as a test, but I'm afraid the tacky-o-meter would react like a cartoon where you hear a loud "sprong", the springs fall out, and a cuckoo falls out lifeless on the ground with its tongue hanging out.

Or we can take our tacky-o-meter to Key West and hold it up to the windows of the tee shirt shops so the tack-o-meter can read what is written on the shirts and contemplate the people who wear them. Again, I'm afraid the tack-o-meter would start to cry and rust out.

The Cult Of -Er

What ever happened to "-er"? I don't know if it is pure, cussed laziness, lack of education, or what, but it is clearly a sign of the times. Remember when people said *harder* or *easier* or *faster* instead of *more hard* or *more easy or more fast*? Or worse *more easier*. Come on, folks, why is this so hard? Even my grandson rates cereal as the *bestest* or the *worstest*, though I'll settle for that. I believe it is a sign of the times that no one uses the -er form of comparatives anymore because they are too lazy to do so. It is a harbinger of our moral and ethical decay, if you ask me.

I've got an idea: let's start the cult of -er. We will all use the comparative forms of words. We can snicker at the folks that say *more this* and *more that*, as we'll be the only ones in the know. We will say to ourselves, "What a clod! What a moron!"

The cult of er will also not add "at" the end of sentences. You will not hear, "Where is he at?" coming from a member.

The cult of er will only use ain't when they are pretending to be Lord Peter Wimsey. I guess the aristocracy in those days were allowed to use ain't, but it was a wink wink kind of thing; they knew it wasn't correct grammar.

I have to say I have been known to break the cult of er rules. I have been reprimanded by my grandson, who is a stickler for good grammar. He has more than once reminded me not to say, "I'm good" When he does that, I suddenly picture the two of us on a heath in England with tweed suits and shotguns under our arms with the pheasants we have bagged and my grandson says, "How are you grandpa?" and I say, "I'm good" and my grandson looks up a me and removes the monocle from his eye and says, "Sorry, old bean it just isn't done. It is well not good" to which I reply "Right ho"

The cult of er. Sounds kind of Egyptian. We can have meetings in secret places and sacrifice a box of Luckier Charms.

Travel Plans

Signs, Signs, Everywhere Signs

So I am on a train in New Haven headed for New York. I am sitting in my seat, and I look over and see a sign that says, "No spitting on this train." Christ, can you believe it? I was just about to let out a huge spit and now I had to freaking hold it. Now I had to get out at the next station to spit.

Just kidding. I have no interest in spitting anywhere, let alone in a train car. But it does raise a number of questions. First, was there a time when spitting was cool and everyone did it? Then I think who is this sign for? Is it for people like me, who have no intention of spitting in the first place, or is it for those that do?

If it is for people that spit, do you really think a sign is going to stop them? Do they get ready for a really great spit, then see that sign and suddenly stop? Seems to me that spitters will spit despite any signs, just as non-spitters will not.

Of course, we all know what it's really about. Some guy spits on the train and he is tossed, as he should be in a rational world. He then hires attorneys Shyster, Shyster, and McCormick who tell the train company, "Hey, you don't have a sign that says no spitting." So the guy is reimbursed for x amount of dollars and the train people have to put up a sign.

But why just in English? Seems to me that it should be in every known language and that it should encompass far more than just spitting. What about peeing and pooping, or picking your nose and rubbing it on the seats? Without a sign, hey, it's a free world.

On my way from Connecticut to Florida via I-95, there is a sign on a major Maryland bridge that says, "No stopping on bridge."

When I saw this, I turned to my wife and said, "Shoot, honey, now we'll have to find somewhere else for our picnic lunch." We had planned to stop on the bridge, spread out a tablecloth, and have lunch. Now this had all been ruined by the sign.

Who was this sign for? If we eliminate non English speaking folks and folks that can't read, we are left with folks who speak English and are not illiterate and need a sign to point out the obvious. I am praying this group is a small percentage of the population and they have decided not to procreate.

Then I say to myself, how did these dolts get a license?

To be absolutely fair, it is possible that some lawyer somewhere decided that a sign is necessary because we really aren't very bright people and can't be blamed for stopping on a bridge when there is no sign.

The tunnel in Maryland, Fort McHenry: I find myself singing "The Star-Spangled Banner" every time I pass through it. Anyway, now there are signs that say, "NO HAZMAT." I was perplexed by this until my wife informed me that this means "No hazardous material." Shoot—now I have to find another way to move that nuclear waste I have in the back of my Rav 4.

I keep picturing potential terrorists with a U-Haul full of dynamite heading for Washington D.C, through the tunnel and they see that sign and say, "Dang it, Leroy, now we have to find another way into the city"

There are also signs in Virginia that say, "Speed monitored by aircraft." I am trying to picture the Commonwealth of Virginia telling some pilot, "Hey, Bob, fly around all day and tell us who is speeding." Virginia must be flush with cash.

mini comas

On Interstate 81 in Pennsylvania, they have signs that indicate that if you are unharmed in a collision, you should move your car off to the side of the road. I have tried to picture this happening: First of all, we are all going faster than the speed limit of 65 or 70 miles per hour on Interstate 81, and I can't really picture an accident in which someone could emerge unharmed, but let's say it did happen.

I just happen to "brush" the rear fender of the car in front of me while going 70 mph. Now what? Do we both get out of the car while all the other cars go speeding by and say, "Hey, Bob, you okay?"—"Sure, Bill, I'm fine. Let's pull our cars off the highway." Sorry, Pennsylvania. It really is hard to picture.

Another sign down the road in one of the Carolinas is for Ava Gardner's house. Do people actually decide to go there? I mean, do you plan it all out, even go to AAA to get the discount tickets and travel brochures?

Every time we pass it, my wife says, "Geez, honey, we missed it again."

"One of these days, honey, when we have more money, we can stop," I reply.

And I keep thinking, isn't the population of people who even know who Ava Gardner was dwindling by the day? Won't there be a point where the pool of potential sightseers who will want to see her house is at zero?

But I suspect that even if you went today, you would probably have to wait until Frank could be located at the local Dairy Queen, where he works on the side, to open the door and show you around.

Further down the road on I-95 is a sign that says, "Decoy Museum." Now this one has some truly interesting possibilities. Of course you know and I know that if you got off at the exit and went to the museum, you could ogle a roomful of dusty old wooden duck decoys.

But what if it was something different? What if you got off to go to the decoy museum only to find that it was just a hologram? A guide would laugh and say, "The real decoy museum is over there."

As you wind your way down I-95 South, not sure if you're in North Carolina or South, you will see a sign that says, "Stonewall Jackson Shrine." I always try to see the deeper meanings in these things. Shrine? Wasn't this a

64

guy who promoted the idea of slavery, body and soul, and even gave his life for that cause? Hmm…shrine doesn't quite do it for me.

If you are interested in shrines, I direct you to downtown Atlanta, Georgia, where you can find the grave of Martin Luther King, Jr. There is an eternal flame and the crypts (husband and wife, which makes it more romantic) are protected from loonies by a pool of water surrounding the crypts. I went to see it once and bowed my head to a great man. His church is nearby.

I waited until the Sunday service was over and asked if I could touch the pulpit where he had preached. I think they thought I was nuts, but they let the white lunatic touch the pulpit. I recommend visiting this area to everyone. He truly was a great man, right up there with Thomas Jefferson, Ben Franklin, and Abraham Lincoln in my book.

When you get further south into Virginia, the exits have multiple signs: one for all the gas stops and names of the stations, one for all the places you can rest your head at night, and one for all the fine food you can get. When you see something you like, you get off at the exit, and there are more signs telling you which direction you should head in and for how far.

It's a totally different story when you come north. I have found that most of the signs have a little stick figure lying on a cot. I assume this means "hotel," or maybe it means "hospital." I'm not sure which, but I'm not sure I would want to go there; those symbols aren't very inviting. The stick man on the cot somehow reminds me of World War I, with its rows of cots and sick people.

I keep trying to picture the hotel that is represented by the stick figure on the cot. Would you really want to stay there? Is that the best they can do with their advertising dollar? A stick man on a cot? Does anyone even remember cots? I do remember rollaways, those foldup beds with springs hanging out. Your parents would get a room, and they would drag out the ol' rollaway for the kids to sleep on. Child abuse.

Food signs in the North are a plate with a fork and knife across the plate. We went to one of these in Pennsylvania. When we sat down, I noticed a young girl with bare feet dancing in front of the jukebox. I thought, Christ, I'm in a remake of *The Last Picture Show*.

My kids were with me, and the menu said you could get honey-dipped chicken. I looked at my kids and said, "Do you know what that means?"

They said they didn't, so I said, "It means that if you order it, the waitress goes back in the kitchen and yells, 'Honey! Dip some chicken.'"

Our table also had the classic plastic cow with milk coming out of her nose and mouth. I find those types of things typical of places that are advertised by a plate, fork, and knife.

The other thing about the North is when you get off and exit at a sign with a stick man on a cot, there is no indication of how far you have to go to find it. It could be a mile; could be ten miles for all you know.

Besides the stick man on a cot for hotels, the plate with a knife and fork for restaurants, and the rather ancient looking gas pump for gas, signs in the Northeast also have a picture of what looks to me to be a Bakelite phone handset. I assume this means you can call somebody if you get off at that exit, but are there really any telephone booths anymore? Unless, Clark Kent needs a place to change or perhaps you have entered the Twilight Zone

Lead in from the TV show Twilight Zone:

"This highway leads to the shadowy tip of reality: you're on a through route to the land of the different, the bizarre, the unexplainable...Go as far as you like on this road. Its limits are only those of mind itself. Ladies and Gentlemen, you're entering the wondrous dimension of imagination. Next stop....The Twilight Zone."

Rod Serling appears and says, "The Hanson's have been travelling for days from Florida to Connecticut. They have been doing this for years. Their trips have always been uneventful until today. Today, inexplicably they have no cell phones and wish to make a call. There is a sign post up ahead with a phone handset indicating a phone. This exit my friends is the Twilight Zone".

I then picture us getting off the exit looking for said phone. We find a deserted gas station off I 95 with a phone booth, the doors opening and closing in the wind. I enter the phone booth to make a call, the operator asks for a deposit of $.50. I deposit the coins and make the call. After several rings I hear, "You can save 15% on your car insurance with Geico". I hang up the phone to make another call, the operator asks for another deposit, I deposit the $.50 and make the call, the phone rings and I hear, "This is Dale Allen's Tattoo and piercing parlor". I hang up becoming more and more desperate. I deposit $.50 more and dial and I hear, "If you are in an injury call Franklin and Franklin for all your legal needs" All goes black.

Why There Are Traffic Jams At Rush Hour

The DMV in every large city hires a bunch of old farts to be at every exit and entrance ramp on every interstate that passes through a city. They are given a signal, and then they all take off at 5 miles per hour at the same time.

I believe it absolutely.

Airlines

So there you are flying from point A to point B. Now, it just so happens that in order to get to point B, you have to stop at point C and board a new plane to point B. You land at point C and come out at Gate A1, and then notice that your flight leaves in half an hour from Gate 2,300,000 G. Do they videotape you running like a madman through the terminals? I imagine some guys sitting in a booth, each with a baloney sandwich and coffee, laughing their asses off as they watch you run from one terminal to another to make your flight.

Remember the days before kiosks when you had to interface with an airline worker in their terminal in order to get a seat assignment? Now remember, you have already bought a ticket from here to there, and you know the departure time and date as well as the estimated arrival.

You would stand in line to get to the counter, and this is what I never understood. They would then ask you where you were going, so you would present your printed documents. Then began the clicking of the keys.

Now personally, I think they were always just typing, "Now is the time for all good men to come to the aid of the party." They would look up at you once in a while as they continue to type, and then ask you what your end destination was. You would answer, and they would merrily type away some more. I mean, they could have written out the whole Bible by this time.

They finally look up after their endless typing and say, "Would you like an aisle seat?" You'd reply, and then they would clack away again for another ten minutes. Maybe they were creating "to do" lists, or a secret dossier on you. They then ask you have luggage and you say, "Yes" and they clack away again, then they say, "What is the final destination for the luggage?" Just kidding, well maybe not. You now "finally' have answered all the questions that were answered before you arrived when you made the reservation and you are free to go on your merry way.

Today when you board the plane the airline staff just call up the passengers by some secret lettering system or by row. Why is it that no matter how many times I've flown, no matter where I go, no matter what letter I get or row I'm in, there are always a gaggle of folks already on the plane when I get on and the overhead is totally jammed with luggage?

I've been thinking it might be easier to bring a blow-up baby along with me; that way, when they say, "People with small children can board now," I could simply blow up my child, whom I'll call Jimmy, get on board, then neatly store Jimmy underneath the seat.

Once you make it to your destination, it's all but impossible to identify your luggage anymore. The ribbon trick was good for a while, but now everyone has a red ribbon, so you go back to examining every piece of luggage, saying to yourself, "Is that mine? It looks like mine. It's black and rectangular and has a pull-out handle so I can roll it conveniently. Wait a minute. all the luggage is black and rolls conveniently. Dang it."

I thought about talking luggage, but then there are too many Bill's and Bob's in the world. Can you imagine the luggage saying, "Hey, Bob, over here"? Half of the luggage would be saying the same thing.

I guess you could program yours to say, "Hey, Ezekiel, over here." That might work. Unless, of course, you have landed in Amish country.

Rental Cars

Here's a good piece of advice: unless you're renting yourself a Lamborghini or Ferrari, and excuse me if you are, you need to pick out the loudest car you can find. Pick purple or green or red. Do not ever pick black, white, gray, or champagne. Why? Because, my friend, every car is black, white, gray, or champagne, so when you park your lackluster rental car at some mall or grocery store, you are never going to find it. But rent yourself a bright yellow car and you won't have much trouble finding it in the supermarket parking lot. You know, I am beginning to think this colored rental car thing is really for people like me that are on the verge of senility.

Hotel Bathrooms

Ever notice how a hotel toilet never clogs? You could throw bricks in there and *whoosh*, right down they go. You go home and try that and you'll spend some interesting time with a mop and a plumber's helper. Why is that? Do hotels get the "special" hotel toilet with the uncloggable drain? Can I get one too or do you have to be a hotel owner? I guess I can see the reasoning here. You can't control the folks that are staying at your hotel and what they are likely to flush down there. But it would have been nice to have one when the kids were growing up.

Places I'd Like To Visit

I'd like to visit the factory that makes scratchy towels for hotels. I have to believe it is one gigantic factory that makes them all. They're all the same size (not quite big enough to really dry yourself) and all the same level of scratchiness (I think you could take your skin off with one of those babies).

I'd be interested in how they get them that scratchy. Do you think they are made by monks? Maybe they got the idea from those scapulars they wear to do penance. However it is done, it is truly an art form. How do they get the towels to all have the same level of scratchiness throughout?

The kicker is that most hotels have a card outlining the cost of said towels. Now you know and I know this is their quaint way of saying, "Steal a scratchy towel and we are going to charge you." I'm trying to picture the people who would want take those towels. Not a pretty picture. You know what would be cool? Go down to the desk at checkout time and tell them you want three of those swell towels, maybe a couple of washrags to go with them. Extra-scratchy, if they can manage.

I'd also like to visit the factory that makes the bedspreads for these same hotels. You know those rich brown and gold bedcovers that are designed in such a way that any dirt or debris on them is camouflaged by their color palate? I wish they would give you a pair of tongs when you check in so you can remove them without actually having to put your fingers on them.

While we're touring, I'd like to visit the place where they make the tiny shampoos and soaps. I suspect they're made in the oak tree where the Keebler elves live. Besides making cookies, they probably also make little bitty bottles of conditioner.

I want to visit the farm where perfect hardboiled eggs are made. The Publix in Naples sells perfect prepackaged hardboiled eggs. Now I don't know about you, but I've tried a million times and consulted many, many cookbooks on the fine art of making hardboiled eggs, and to this day, I don't think I have ever produced a complete set of perfect hardboiled eggs. I end up with dimples and holes and pieces missing.

But the ones in Publix's are absolutely perfect. Where do they get them from? Is there a special Publix's chicken farm?

I'd like to visit a dirt farm where they bag up dirt to sell in Home Depot and Lowes. I keep picturing the guy who thought of this, chuckling away as he fills another plastic bag with the rarest of dirt, the crème de la crème of dirt. I still haven't found out what makes it such great dirt. Does he have to create it from certain rocks or seashells; spending hours eroding it away into the finest dirt money can buy?

I know my wife will not plant any new plant unless we have a bag of dirt. Do you think the plants around the new plant grumble when they see us put a shovelful of this black gold in before planting the new addition? Do they say, "Well, isn't he special? Gets the good dirt." Funny thing is, when summer hits here in Naples, the flowers are usually all dead anyway, despite the fabulous dirt.

I wouldn't be surprised to find out that in today's world all of our dirt is imported. Hell, we don't make anything anymore anyway. The stuff probably comes from China.

I want to visit a garden hose factory. You've got to give those people credit. I don't know how they get those hoses wrapped up like that, 'cause you know hoses are really kind of alive. I don't know if those people have to beat them into submission or use some kind of sedative. All I know is that once you get one home and let it loose, all you can hope for is a hopeless tangle of hose when you want to roll it back up. It simply can't be done. The hose twists and turns until you finally give up.

And when you want to use the hose, it will grab onto anything it can to stop from being dragged around. It will hook itself on any root or bush or birdfeeder it can find. And don't try to tell me it's the way I am dragging it; oh no, my friend, that hose is laughing at you all the way along. It loves it when you have something on a porch or deck it can grab hold of and topple over, and when you finally get it to the point where you can water whatever it is you are watering, no water comes out. You look back, and it has twisted itself into a tight knot to shut the water flow off.

So hats off to those folks at hose factories. Unsung heroes, if you ask me. And here's to the makers of scratchy towels and hotel bed spreads and especially to the dirt farmers everywhere who pack the dirt in those flimsy plastic bags that leak dirt all over the back of your RAV4.

Family Matters

My Mother

My mother was the smartest person who ever lived. I grew up during the Cold War and we lived near the Timken Roller Bearing plant. Well! I'll tell you, you can't fight a war without roller bearings, so our little town was *numero uno* on the Ruskies' list of hits. As an aside, years later, I was in Spain in a bar talking to a Russian. Turns out that not only did he not know where the Timken Roller Bearing plant was he didn't know where the state of Ohio was; go figure.

In school, we would get under our desks during periodic air raid drills. I remember telling my mother about this, and she said, "Well, then there's nothing to worry about. Just carry a school desk over your head at all times." I didn't think it was funny at the time, but now I find it a total scream.

Our neighbors began building bomb shelters back in the fifties and stocking them with huge cans that said "CD" on the side; I think they were some kind of canned meat. Of course I wanted to know why we weren't building one too.

My mother replied, "Every May Day, the Russians haul that moth-eaten rocket out of storage and prance it around, then put it away again until next year. They have nothing. This is the greatest country on the face of the earth, and trust me, we will stop them, even if we have to do it in their own backyard."

My mother believed that despite everything, America was the greatest country. No matter what differences we had, we would always pull together when times got tough. She believed that we collectively knew that we were all Americans, that Americans stood for something, and that we would all stand together no matter what. I miss her very much.

I have always had trouble with time. I used to ask my mother why she didn't go to Washington's funeral. She would patiently explain that the two of them had been alive at different times, and I would go away to mull this over for a while, but as I said, I had trouble understanding time. Finally, after getting tired of trying to make me understand time, she said she had been busy doing wash and couldn't make it. I thought this was insensitive of her, but I accepted it.

In first grade, we had a music teacher named Miss Jones. She divided the class up into canaries and crows. Guess who was the only crow in the whole class? You got it.

I was devastated. I went home and told my mother that I was a crow.

She looked at me and said, "Real men are crows. They certainly aren't canaries." I have wallowed in my crowiness ever since. The world is full of canaries and it needs more crows.

How Did My Parents Do It?

Was there really any life before plastic garbage bags? I think back to when I was smaller to try and remember how my parents could have lived without them.

What did our parents put things in? I use plastic bags for practically anything. They are the de facto means of putting things into other things. Maybe they didn't keep as much stuff back then, but where did our parents put their things? What did they put sandwiches in, for example? Or weren't there any? Seems to me I had a sandwich as a young lad, though I think they were in paper bags.

How did our parents get garbage out? Is it possible that like with the pyramids and the heads on Easter Island, extraterrestrials interceded to dispose of the garbage for our parents? I vaguely remember lining metal trashcans with newspaper; I also remember what a mess it was and how it was full of maggots in the summer. But then I think, Hey, maggots gotta live. That whole lifecycle ended when we went to plastic bags.

I was pumping gas the other day when I slid my credit card into the slot and it didn't work. Christ on a Crutch, as my sainted ma used to say. I had to walk all the way into the gas station to get my freaking card to work.

But then I think back to when I was little and when my parents would drive into the local gas station. You would have to wait for an attendant to come out to pump the gas, and then he would check your oil and air pressure. God, how did they do it? How could they spend that much time filling up with gas? It would drive me crazy.

I also remember driving to New York with my parents on the Ohio and Pennsylvania turnpike. If you were hungry, your choices were Howard Johnson. If you preferred something a little more elegant, there was always Howard Johnson, or for a change of pace, you would head for Howard Johnson. That was it: Howard Johnson or nothing. And to top it all off, you had to gag down Ho-Jo cola, which was some kind of fake Coca-Cola. Just how did they live in those primitive times?

Did our parents really live a great deal of their lives without paper towels? The evidence seems to indicate that they did, but I don't believe it. I believe that when man crawled out of the primordial sea, he was clutching ether a roll of Bounty paper towels, perhaps Brawny.

I personally do not believe life on this planet was ever possible without paper towels. It would seem that they really didn't exist until modern times, but I think if you dig deep enough, you will find the evidence: man and paper towels evolved at the same time.

Growing Up Absurd

I realize now that if I had been born today and did the same things I had done as a kid, I would surely be put away. People would shake their heads and wonder what was wrong with my parents.

Family Matters

From an early age, I loved making gunpowder and blowing things up. I loved blowing up bottles and cans and model cars. I was always trying to perfect the recipe of sulfur, carbon, and potassium nitrate that Jerry Marlowe, the local pharmacist, would sell me. Thanks, Jer; today, he would be in prison with me.

I never could master the fuse, but I discovered that if I connected a pen spring to two wires, then attached it to my train transformer, then packed a model car with my homemade gunpowder, stuck the spring in the car, and plugged in the transformer, I got a most satisfying *kaboom.*

I also somehow discovered that if you mixed iodine crystal with ammonia and let it dry it made the most amazing powder for bingo bombs. Or better yet, I could spread it on my sister's room floor, listen for her to walk in, and *snap, crackle,* and *pop.* Hysterical stuff.

I used to stuff my clothes with newspaper to make dummies. My mother used to have a coffee klatch on Sundays where ladies would sit in the kitchen, drink coffee, and chitchat. There was a big old window in the kitchen looking out into the backyard. But the really cool thing was that right above the kitchen, there was a porch on the second floor that connected to my room.

One time, I waited for the coffee klatch to get underway, then threw the dummy over the side of the second floor porch so it would pass by the kitchen window and let out a bloodcurdling scream. Those ladies were never the same.

One day, my best friend Dave and I were playing outside when I had this brainstorm. I tied a rope around his waist and pulled it up through the back of his shirt. I then took another piece of rope and looped it around his neck before connecting it to the rope coming out the back of his shirt.

We then staged a fake hanging from the limb of a tree in the backyard. I have to admit, Dave played his part well; he was really swinging from his waist, but appeared to have been hung. I ran into the house and told my mom there had been a terrible accident. She ran out. It was one of the few times my mother was not amused.

I know I know you are shaking your head wondering how I didn't end up on *48 Hours Investigates,* but I swear, despite all of the nutty things I did,

I never ever once thought about hurting anyone. The firecrackers were just to hear the boom. The other stuff, well, that was just nuts. It never once occurred to me to fire my BB gun at anyone, for example. Even when I got to use my friend's dad's shotgun, it was only to shoot clay pigeons.

But things changed once we had Columbine. How does this stuff happen? I have my own theory, crazy as it is. I believe that lawyers got together with some scientists to develop a drug that would reduce what I call the Jiminy Cricket factor: "Always let your conscience be your guide." The drug would suppress the inner voice that tells you right from wrong. The idea being that without that people would not feel responsible for their own actions and would sue for any possible cause whether it was finding out you can't shred your fish through a paper shredder or use your lawn mower to file your nails.

The first experiments were in South LA. Too much of the drug and we ended up with the Bloods and the Crips. A little refinement and it hit Middle America, leading to Columbine and other shootings in the Midwest. I think they have refined the drug now so we are at the level of, "Sue that bastard."

Hey, that could make a really good reality show.

High Tech

Internet

The Internet to me is really Pandora's Box from mythology. Once she opened it, every horrible thing in the universe started pouring out of it.

Our enemies now have instant access to each other to plan our demise. Every fool, dolt, and idiot can write anything about anything or anybody, and it doesn't have to a grain a truth to it; no one will call you out on it, so you can anonymously and gutlessly rave on and on, spewing whatever kind of crap you want. Pedophiles come crawling out of the woodwork through the Internet to find young boys and girls. Child pornography is thriving because of all the slimebags who download it and distribute it on the Internet. There are scams galore to steal your money or your identity.

Those scams on the Internet—wowsers. They run so deep it's like peeling back the layers of an onion. Take fat ads. I just found out that fat people will sell their pictures to whomever, and then give them the rights to crop these photos in any way they wish so that advertisers can prove that their magic diet elixir works for old Betty there who lost fifty pounds. Well, let's say she lost fifty pounds courtesy of Photoshop.

Here's another one: you set up a consumer agency that supposedly rates products, though you are really being paid by one company that is trying to sell their worthless product. You have a bunch of phony people testify that this product is the greatest thing since sliced bread. You then pay a respected web-site like CNN, or Yahoo, or Weather Channel to post it. Then you say, "Hey, posted on one of these websites. Must be true". Not.

And then there's Facebook. Okay, okay, I know I'm in the minority here. There is no life without Facebook, but doesn't it bother you even a little bit that you are letting the whole world know everything there is to know about you? Oh, so only your friends can know, right? It's impossible to hack Facebook? Okay—dream on.

Sure, the Internet is a vast source of information, but sometimes I wonder if it's worth it. My son and I have this continuing argument. I say that the Internet leads to brains of mush. True, you can find out anything you want to, but then you don't have to think about anything. You don't have to cudgel your brain to come up with anything. Have a question about a movie? Look it up on the Internet. Can't figure out the answer to a crossword? Look it up.

My son says I'm totally wrong, and that the Internet frees you up for other intellectual pursuits. I asked him if he could google that to see if it is true.

As an aside, I was watching a cartoon with my grandson. The cartoon was a series and I had missed a lot of the episodes so I kept interrupting and asking him who was who and what was what and he finally looked at me and said, "I'm not google, grandpa". Smart aleck.

I Need More Apps

Unlike the civilized state of Florida, Connecticut insists on charging you a nickel for cans and bottles in the hope that you will bring them back to a store to get your nickel back. Now ordinarily, I wouldn't give it two cents' worth of my time and would throw the cans in the recycle bin. But my grandson lets me know in no uncertain terms the "vast" amount of money I am wasting (like grandma like grandson). So I told him that we would go together so he could put the cans in the machine and collect the booty.

High Tech

But I need an app that tells me that this is the day someone has decided they are going to haul in every can and bottle they've been collecting for the last six months. It never fails.

We walk into the bottle return, and someone is there with carts full of cans. I want to just throw mine in with their piles and leave, but my grandson insists we do things ourselves, so we go away and attempt it another day.

I want this new app to just flash a warning that someone like that is heading over with a million cans. Can't be that hard.

I need an app that listens to a politician, and then comes up with a true or false reading. Well, maybe that would really be the same as making an app out of that Magic 8 Ball you had as a kid. You would ask it questions, turn it over, and it would say, "Better not tell you now."

I want an app that gives me "pithy" things to say at parties. Maybe an Oscar Wilde app.

As I grow older and the weight doesn't come off as easily, I have actually begun to read the contents of what I am eating. I weigh the various merits of a bag of bite-size Snickers over Mounds. I need an app that reads these nutritional facts and either displays a smiley face or a face with a tongue hanging out.

I need an app that runs all the time, listens to what I am saying, and says, "Stop, you fool!" at appropriate times. This would be especially useful when I'm saying something to my spouse that will end up with her giving me the cold shoulder and me doling out a number of "What's the matter's? What did I do's?" before I know what it was that I said.

Religious Matters

Naked Women, Pecans, And Jesus

When I travel south through the Carolinas and Georgia, I call this the land of pecans, naked woman, and Jesus. Every so many miles, you see signs for women that bare it all, and right beside those signs are other signs with various sayings about how there is no life without Jesus. Couple that with the endless stands selling peanuts and pecans and I think you can get my drift. I know this is total blasphemy, but I picture Jesus sitting in one of those roadside bars with a naked girl on each arm and a bowl of unshelled peanuts.

As you travel down I-95 into the South, you also see signs for Adult Superstores. Are there shopping carts so you can load up on your favorite movies, whips and chains, and rubber items? Do they have tastings like they do at Costco or Sam's Club? I imagine a woman saying, "Would you like to try the edible cherry panties, three to a pack?" Do they do demos like in...Oh, never mind.

I picture church goers on a Sunday planting three more crosses on some hill overlooking the interstate, maybe a new billboard saying, "Without the lord, there shall be no mercy." And then when the sermon is over, Earl and Wanda say, "Hey, let's head over to The Lion's Den and pick up some whips, maybe some edible panties for dinner."

Afterlife

I was leaving Costco the other day when I saw a bunch of coffins. Well, sample coffins, kind of. What you see are end pieces of coffins kind of glued to the wall and around the glued coffin pieces are pictures of smiling folks making a selection. Under the pictures are slogans that say, "Nonthreatening" and "being prepared for the future". Nonthreatening? I'll tell you what, if my wife comes home and shows me the coffin she bought for me, I am darn well going to feel threatened (unless you were a vampire, in which case I guess it's kind of romantic).

Anyway, you can pick out different colors and motifs like a cross on all the corners. The display says that the inside of the coffin is comfortable and can be adjusted. Adjusted for whom? I mean, it's not like you're in a hospital bed and they're going to ask if they can raise you up a bit. You'd be dead, so I doubt you would care that much.

Besides, I'll let you in on a little secret: when I was growing up in Dover, Ohio, we lived near the Meese Funeral Home, and Peggy Meese let me lie in a coffin once. Gotta tell ya', even if I were dead, those coffins would be uncomfortable. They spend most of the money on the outside.

So I'm standing there holding up the line at Costco, trying to get out of the store (the coffin display is in the aisle that leads out of the building), when I start thinking. If I buy one, then what? I mean, what do you do with it until you need it? Can they make it into a big beer keg? Now that would be a conversation piece. Or maybe a bookcase; you could fill it with Stephen King novels. Or maybe you could just haul it out into the front yard on Halloween and jump out at the kiddies.

I couldn't resist, so I took a sales brochure. All of the coffins have names. The most expensive is the *Kentucky Rose*—I'm not sure why that is. I have yet to call the reps on this—but there is also a *Brian*. Who is *Brian*, and how did he get a casket named after him? I'm sorry, but that sounds a little effeminate to me. They also have the *Morgan*, which kind of has a swashbuckler, pirate-y kind of name, as if it should have a skull and crossbones on it, with parrots on the side. Maybe it says, "Arrr, matey!" when the bereaved pass by.

Then I think, Okay, so I make my choice and send in my money. Does the coffin then come to Costco for me to pick up? Personally, I would be very disappointed if it didn't. I want to load it on the cart and have them look at my slip as I'm leaving as if to say, "Sir, I hope you paid for that thing. Can you please open the lid so we can see that you didn't slide an LCD TV or bottles of wine in there?"

But then what? I don't think my Rav 4 is big enough to push it all the way in. Do they give you string to hold the back doors closed?

But then it dawned on me. You could mount it on top of your car like one of those cargo holders. It would be perfect. That way, you get both a conversation piece and something to haul things around in until you need it.

Then, when you finally do go, you just need to make arrangements to have someone hoist you up and into it and drive it off to the cemetery. Pretty slick, if you ask me.

Hell

I have a somewhat different view of hell. Yeah, I believe that there are a number of concentric circles, one inside another and the closer you get to the innermost circle, the worse it is for you. But I disagree with all that stuff about hanging you upside-down over the heat, or even that it is full of insurance salesman. No, the inner circle of hell is a woman's clothing store that goes on for all eternity.

There is no end to the racks of clothes or the expanse of the petite section. The dressing rooms are all full, and the lines to make purchases are endless. My idea is that if you end up there, you will have to follow some woman around the store forever. The woman will look at everything, try everything on, and never buy a thing. I shudder at the thought, because I have seen what it can do to a man after a few short minutes.

I have followed my wife through many clothes stores. Oh God, it is desperately dull. I feel all the energy flowing out of me and onto the floor as we move through the racks of clothes. I see the other poor suckers like me. They follow along, carrying the clothes that are going to be tried on, wearing that glazed-over look or looking like a deer in the headlights.

No, but it's worse than either of those; it's pure zombification. It turns ordinary men into mindless bag-holding zombies. The Haitians didn't use chicken blood and incantations to make zombies. They made the guys walk through a women's clothing store for three days straight. Trust me; no man would ever recover from such a thing. The difference in hell is that the devil makes you tell your wife that you are enjoying the shopping experience and you would love to continue.

Christ, clothes to me are a Dickies t-shirt, any color, a pair of Levi 505 jeans, and maybe some black Converse tennis shoes for a *Sunday go to meetin'*. Men can try on a dozen pair of pants in one minute; women take hours. When women go back to the fitting room, is there a bridge game going on that we don't know about?

Women go through each rack. Oh God, don't you know what you want? Not only that, but do you ever notice how they jump from rack to rack? You think they are done with one, than they jump back to the one they were just looking at. Then they pick something up and say, "Do you like it?" Geez O Weez.

Then they look at you and say, "Don't you care how I look?" Geez, you already know how you look. Why do you need me for this?

And then when she finally says, "I am ready to go," you feel yourself coming back to life. You are almost skipping down the aisle. You can see the outside of the mall. You can see the door to the exit. You can almost feel the fresh air on your face. You even take being sprayed by women's cologne as you pass the makeup department.

Then she moves sideways and says, "Let me just take a quick look at the shoes." Oh, God, just shoot me.

There's another section of hell where you can get all the sushi you want. You can also get all the "easy-open" packets of soy sauce you want. But here's the catch.

During orientation, the devil lets you know that you will have no scissors or knives to use on the easy-open packets, and if you are caught using your teeth, you will either be sent to the endless clothes store or will have to watch Nancy Grace and Jane Velez-Mitchell forever.

In another section of hell, Glenn Beck and Keith Olbermann debate the issues of the day together. While you are listening to those two, schoolmarm Rachel Maddow is rapping you on the knuckles with a ruler reminding you how utterly uninformed you are and how worthless your opinion is, because, if you just knew the facts like she does, you wouldn't be so cussedly stupid. I'll take the clothes store every time.

I think the devil has quite the sense of humor.

How Did We Get So Freaking Shallow?

My personal opinion is that God destroyed Sodom and Gomorrah because the people there had reached a level of shallowness that not even God could put up with. Now I think God is looking around again to select a new site for some biblical levels of destruction.

He has many, many options to choose from. He could naturally pick most of California, and I think everyone would agree that he had made a pretty wise choice. But just like when people are trying to figure out where to hold the summer Olympics, I am holding out for my own personal favorite and trying to get God to give it some consideration: my choice is for God's next wrath-filled bender is South Beach in Miami, Florida.

My son hails from South Beach, though through no fault of his own; he just happens to have a job there. I am hoping God gives him a pass, but the rest of the town—woo boy. My wife and I have visited him several times, and this is my take. South Beach is the land of expensive bottled water, phrases like, "love you, mean it", and little dogs. Everyone has a little dog. I don't think they have them because they like little dogs particularly, but because little dogs have become a sign of sophistication, which totally escapes me. Anyway, it is my belief that if something goes wrong with your little dog, you pitch it in the nearest trash bin and get yourself another little dog.

As a result, South Beach is also the land of dog poop. No one can be bothered to pick it up. Now the reason that the rich and famous, who love South Beach, never see it is because, 1. They are wandering around at night when you can't see the dog poop, and 2. They have limos to drive them from point A to point B, thus avoiding all the intervening dog poop.

Don't get me wrong. The art deco buildings are spectacular, but I'm afraid the days of Lord Peter Wimsey and ultimate class are gone, replaced by women who take selfies of their boobs and then pass them around for others to see on the beach. I can only hope that God leaves the buildings and turns the shallow folks into a pillar of salt so long as it is some kind of fancy kosher salt or sea salt or perhaps even Himalayan.

I can just imagine the whole thing: as God prepares to get rid of South Beach, some announcer on CNN says, "Tonight on Anderson Cooper 360, Anderson interviews God over the coming destruction of South Beach."

I can hear that interview now:

Anderson:

So, Lord, why South Beach?

God:

Call me God, Anderson. Lord sounds so formal. Well, as you know, I haven't done this in some time. I'm slow to burn, but *man*, the shallowness of some people has really started to give me a pain.

Anderson:

Understood, God, but why did you choose South Beach? Why not Los Angeles or Washington?

God:

Well, Anderson, the problem with Los Angeles is that the shallowness is spread all over the place. You'd have to wipe out endless pockets of people, and that's tough because I've found fire and brimstone to be tricky stuff to work with. It kind of unpredictable where it hits no pinpoint accuracy with the stuff, but South Beach has an enormous concentration of shallowness that is perfect for raining down fire and brimstone. As for Washington DC...Well, Anderson, I was really after shallow this time. If I had been going after *stupid*, then Washington would have been at the top of the list.

Anderson:

But God, what about just a symbol of shallowness like changing a reality star into a pillar of salt or raining horny toads down on some politician involved in some sex scandal?

God:

Well Anderson, while changing a reality star into a pillar of salt seems like a good idea, can you imagine the production value of that? As for the horny toads, there is a certain irony in that, but we had selected South Beach long ago, and heaven is just like any other company with its endless committees. Plus, once you get Jesus and Mohammed in the same room-geez! Things take forever.

Anderson:

Well, God, I hope the destruction goes well

God:

Thank you, Anderson. We hope to launch a successful strike against shallowness.

Jesus And Mohammed

Do you suppose those two guys confer in heaven? Man, those two are probably shaking their heads at us. Jesus can't get past how shallow and phony we've become, and Mohammed can't get over how crazy the Al Qaeda and Taliban folks are. Do they ever look at each other and say, "Wow, everyone is a loon."

I think it would be great if someone could come up with holograms of them that appear in the sky to say, "Hey, knock it off or else."

Alien Stories

Alien Taste

Ever notice that aliens have a penchant for people with those hunting hats with flaps, caught sucking on a piece of wheat with a mouth full of gold and silver? They appear to have a penchant for hicks from the back woods. I suppose it is so they don't attract too much attention or maybe the aliens are teaching these folks about crop circles.

If it were me and I was an alien and I was looking for someone to examine, it would be Angelina Jolie and not some guy from the backwoods. I guess there is no accounting for alien taste.

Aliens Come To Saint Croix

My wife and I recently took a trip to Saint Croix in the Virgin Islands. We stayed at an inn at the tippy-top of a hill overlooking Christianstaad and the harbor. The inn has a balcony where you can sit and drink wine and do nothing.

This was all very nice, but then we got to thinking how all these homes got up in these hills. Who built them? Was it some prehistoric group like the Incas or the Aztecs who had an unlimited supply of slaves to move the cement blocks up the hill? It certainly couldn't have been done by the people currently living there.

We wracked our brains, and the only thing we could think of that made sense was that aliens came and levitated the stuff up the hills. In fact, since homes are still being built there, I suspect that there was some deal that was made with the aliens. I suppose when the time comes when you want to buy a home, the alien contractors come knocking.

I wonder if you get a choice. I mean, do you get a better deal depending on what planet they're from? I guess they inevitably try to fit you in between flying over New Mexico and trampling down fields in England.

Lunatic Fringe

Serial Killers

How does it happen, and why do they all seem to be from the good old US of A? I mean, did Jeffery Dahmer wake up one day and say, "Hmm, I am feeling rather peckish, but I'm tired of pork and chicken."

When Ted Bundy was growing up, did his parents notice that he kept ripping out the front seat of his toy Volkswagen beetle? Did he limp around and ask little girls for help with his schoolbooks?

Did BTK's mom ever say, "Hey, BTK, stop putting those plastic sandwich bags over your sister's Barbie dolls?"

Is there a standard age for becoming a serial killer, kind of like when you can vote or drink alcohol? I mean, does someone think, "Okay, now I'm going to go out and kill a bunch of people for no reason," but then stop when they realize they are only sixteen?

I suppose it has more to do with living at home. Your mom would probably notice the bloody clothes you keep leaving out for her to wash. Dead giveaway.

Maybe there is something to be said for becoming so freaking fat. I suppose it is more difficult for a serial killer to kill when they keep huffing and puffing as they try to grab someone, and then shove both the victim and their own big butt into a car.

Tips For Disposing Of Your Spouse

1. Don't hire someone to do it for you. Times have changed, my friend. Once upon a time, you could trust someone to do a nice, neat job for you and never hear from them again. There was a type of integrity to your basic hired killer that just isn't there anymore.

   Now they are either constantly calling your cell to tell you what a wonderful job they did, or they are sitting in a bar talking it over with the stranger sitting beside them.

   Either way, you go to jail.

2. You know that PC you used to look at websites that tell you how to make an untraceable poison or how to strangle someone without leaving marks? Or those phony suicide letters you typed up to lay on the body?

   No, no, no. You must either format your hard drive, which will certainly catch the attention of even the dullest policeman, or have two PCs. Your backup PC should have a browser history full of searches for romantic getaways, what to buy your spouse for their birthday, and letters of undying love. Keep this one around for the police.

3. Don't shop at Walmart for the rope, tape, and hammer, or anything else you'll need to do the job. They have video surveillance like you wouldn't believe.

   If you must, please, at least pay in cash. Geez, don't even think of using your credit card.

4. It is bad form to open a double indemnity insurance policy the day or even the week before your spouse is offed. Trust me, it piques the police's interest. If insurance is your motive, then you need to spend

a minimum of two years waiting and have a policy ready for both partners.

5. If you must bludgeon your spouse, then please dispose of your clothes. Don't just go home, throw the sneakers in the closet, and wash the clothes. No, no, no! You must have seen enough *Forensic Files* to know they will find some of your spouse on you.

6. Do not carry a cellphone. I know how badly you want to call your lover to tell them all is well, but, friend, it puts you right at the scene. Very bad form; it just isn't done.

7. If you plan on hiding the body in a rental space, you really do need to keep up with the payments.

8. If you decide to bury the body in your basement, then you can't simply decide to move as soon as you're done. Believe it or not, someone will discover the body. I know it's hard to believe, but just take the insurance money and add on a new deck rather than using it as a down payment on a new house.

9. If you are meeting with your lover before the big event, please use cash when you get gas or go out for a meal to discuss the upcoming disposal.

10. If this is your second or third time at this, good for you; perhaps you followed some of my simple tips. But I beg you not to use the same method more than once. Your spouse "accidentally drowning in the spa" might work once, but believe me, the police will take notice if it happens a second time.

Lunatic Fringe

Spice it up. If it was spa drowning the first time, then make it an accidental shooting or poisoning the next.

If you follow these few tips, I believe you will have a safe and happy disposal.

Useful Inventions (Well, Useful To Me)

Self-Cleaning Fridge

Though my ma was one of the smartest people I ever met, she did have some quirks that I myself have inherited. She saved all our leftovers, for one. Didn't matter what it was; it could be a single pea, or maybe a dollop of mashed potatoes. I'm thinking it had something to do with living through the Depression. She would carefully wrap it up in Reynolds wrap and stow it away in the fridge, thinking that she would find some use for it sometime.

Of course, that day would never come, and eventually she would have to unwrap it. I can tell you, the Hansons cornered the market on the makings of penicillin. I used to give the green and purple mossy stuff a name like Fred or Bob. Mold doesn't make a very good pet, but at least it was interesting.

Anyways, my mom would have to throw that stuff away and start over, but here is my big idea:

I want a refrigerator that has one of those self-cleaning slide mechanisms like they have on stoves. When I select *self-clean* on the fridge, it would incinerate all the stuff I didn't want to open. When the cycle was over, everything inside would be nice and fresh. No need to stack Arm & Hammer baking soda in the old fridge.

Or what about this? When I open the fridge, I want it to say, "Bill, that bacon's about to go."

Or better yet, it could figure out a recipe based on what I have and tell me what I could make. "Hey Bill, got a great recipe for a single pea, some mashed potatoes, and leftover spaghetti."

Grocery Bags

I want my groceries to be levitated to my house. I no longer want to make the agonizing decision between clogging the earth with more plastic by choosing plastic or being responsible for destroying another tree by choosing paper.

I know, I know; buy a cloth bag and remember to take it with you. Our house is full of cloth bags. I punish myself every time I go to the store and forget the cloth bag by buying another one. I now have more cloth bags then plastic bags.

No, I want my groceries to go with me through some kind of anti-gravity device; no more bags.

Hair Removal

I want something that picks up wet hair strands from the shower walls, bathroom floors, or sinks. Okay, you can argue that a sponge would pick them all up, but then what? Try scraping them off of the sponge. You know I'm right—it's impossible. But the amazing thing is, if you rub the sponge on your shiny clean sink, there they are again. Call David Copperfield.

GPS

I know GPS's are relatively new as far as inventions go, but I simply cannot live without mine. I even have trouble going to the grocery store. I keep thinking it will come up with an alternate route through some time warp that will get me there faster. I do have some improvements that I'd like to see, however.

My GPS currently speaks in a woman's voice, saying things like, "Please follow the highlighted route." I want a sexy voice that says things like, "Come on, baby, don't you want to follow me down the road?"—"Why don't you turn here, handsome?"—"Why don't we go back to your place?"—"Mmm, I like it that way."

How about a GPS that can pick a restaurant for you based on current deals or whatever you feel like having? Or even better, there should be one that can take a reading of your weight and say, "Sorry, you can't go there tonight."

Or how about a horror-themed GPS that takes you to a deserted farm inhabited by some deranged killer?

I guess that would only be good once.

Shredders

You know, I kind admire the person who thought of the shredder, but the idea also kind of gives me the creeps. Before the shredder was invented, I picture hoards of people at landfills going through my trash to find out everything they could about me. I don't want people to know I am not getting Geico insurance for the hundred millionth time, nor that I do not need any more subscriptions to *Food Illustrated*.

My shredder has little "do not do this" pictures on top, little icons in circles with a line through them. Some of them I get, but I think they really should include a booklet for me to read, and then shred.

There is a picture of a tie, but somehow I can only see this happening if your wife finds out you are seeing someone else. ("Honey," she would say. "Can you come here for a minute?") There is also a picture of a fish; I don't think it would be that easy to push a fish through there, but obviously, someone did.

Then there is picture of a child. Now, I've gotten mad at my kids before, but shredding? Wood chipper, maybe. Do the job right.

Lastly, there is an aerosol can. I'm lost on that one. Someone write me and let me know.

Environmentally Friendly

Raise your hand if you have ever bought one of those light bulbs that last thirty years, hoping to save energy and do the right thing.

Keep your hand raised if that same bulb burned out in one or two years.

Okay, okay. Now keep your hand raised if you have the receipt from the store where you bought it so you can go back and say, "What the hey?"

I lit enough farts in college to know the potential for using fart gas. Hey, I'm not saying it's going to light up New York, but why not use it for heating your home? I can't see why we can't rig toilets to collect the farts then use them to heat water for showers, or maybe even heat your pool.

Can you imagine calling your fart experts when you run dry? They would come to your house and fart up a storm for a price, and away you go. Think of the boon this would be for broccoli farmers? Heating, cooling, and improved health to boot.

Why don't they hook up the treadmills at the local gym to a generator that produces power for the building? I'll bet there are lots of folks willing to run their hearts out to keep the lights going. It would be a challenge: reduce weight and save electricity. Can't get any better than that.

Healthcare

Medical Credit Card

Okay, okay, here's my idea. The insurance companies should hand out medical credit cards. For every dollar you spend on gas, food, or whatever, you get medical points. You too can earn enough points, minus service charges, to pay for a colonoscopy or a prostate exam, or maybe a prescription for Lipitor!

Insurance companies will make billions on credit cards, and we'll all get medical care. Everyone wins. Whaddya think?

Drugs

I want the drug companies to come up with a drug that has nothing but side effects. It doesn't do anything, just causes side effects.

I can imagine the commercial for this new drug. "Side effects include…"

1. Delusions and schizophrenic episodes
2. Projectile vomiting
3. Six-day diarrhea, followed by two months of constipation
4. Heart attacks
5. Loss of hearing and blindness

6. Sudden urge to call a lawyer
7. An irresistible urge to cover your body with tattoos
8. Overwhelming desire to drive 140 mph on Alligator Alley or 35 on Shadowlawn
9. Voices in your head urging you to tell corny jokes like asking someone if their noses run and their feet smell then saying, "You're built upside down" and laughing hysterically.
10. Sudden urge to call Ron Popeil and order your 10th set it and forget it rotisserie

Take as directed. One pill in the evening, and, if you wake up in the morning, take another.

Whatever Happened To...

Ring Around The Collar

When I was growing up, one of the worst things that could befall anyone was ring around the collar. "Those dirty rings. You try soaking them out, scrubbing them out."—Picture the totally desperate housewife agonizing over the collar of her husband's shirt. But then, when all was lost, the hapless housewife is saved by someone introducing her to Wisk. You pour some on the ring, and then bingo, no more ring around the collar.

But all of a sudden, just like the Bubonic Plague, ring around the collar disappeared. Where did it go? Did husbands finally start washing their necks, or was it some kind of disease that was quietly eliminated with fluoridated water? Inquiring minds want to know.

Being Fresh

What happened to douching? I remember ads that would tell women that if they weren't douching, they were utterly unclean. Women would dance down the beach in some flimsy outfit, which indicated that they were douching and smelled fab.

Somewhere along the line, women started smelling good again without having to douche. What happened? How come? Again, I can only put it down to fluoridated water, or maybe the Big Mac.

Unruly Hair

When I was growing up, every man's hair was a mess. You couldn't go anywhere without dousing yourself with Wildroot, or "a little dab'll do ya'" of Brylcreem, or squeezing on some Top Brass. Wasn't it Barbara Feldon on a bear rug for that stuff? When did all of our hair go straight? Where did all the cowlicks go? I suffered most of my life with them and plastered them down with Wildroot. Again must be something in the water that eliminated them or maybe kids get a shot, I don't know what killed off all the cowlicks, but the world is a better place without them.

Typewriters

What do suppose happened to them all? Were they all swallowed up in a vortex like the Pinto? I mean, one minute you had an Underwood on your desk, and then next minute you had a PC with a word processor. Where did they all go?

You know, I had one, but I don't remember what happened to it. One day I was clacking away on it, and the next I had a PC with spellcheck. I had this kind of aqua-colored Corona typewriter. I thought it was very cool.

But one day I had it and the next day it was gone. I don't remember throwing it out. Another coma, I suppose. Well, we do know where one of them went, the guy that created the scale of evil on T.V.

Parting Thoughts

Sometimes I imagine the past as living in a house, all safe and cozy.

Then there was a knock at the door. We said, "Who's there?" No one answered, but the knocking continued.

We opened the door a crack, and a lawyer put his foot in the threshold so we couldn't get it shut again. The lawyer then told us that we were not responsible for anything, and we should be suing anyone we could for everything we could. We said, "Go away", but they didn't go away and everyone was doing it so we shrugged and gave in.

A while later, there came another knock at the door, and we said, "Who's there?" No one answered, but the knocking continued.

We opened the door a crack, and the Internet blew through the space in the doorframe. We loved it. You could find out almost anything, communicate with people with similar interests, start a business, or blog your little hearts out about anything you wanted. It was great.

But then we noticed that Internet was stealing our identities, crashing our computers, selling us all kinds of snake oil to enrich Nigerian scam artists while pedophiles crawled out from under every rock. It was like the Freudian ID had grown while the SUPEREGO had shrunk to the point where people felt nothing about trashing other people anonymously, gutlessly, and without proof. Internet bullying, child pornography...we began to wonder whether it was all worth it

Later, there came another knock on the door. We said, "Who is it?" and a group of people said, "It's The Media. Let us in."

Parting Thoughts

We let them in and found that they wanted to talk and talk and talk about nothing in particular. They wanted to take "who cares" issues and expand them into worldwide concerns. We discovered that they all had their own biases, but didn't care a hoot if they let them show.

Later, there was another knock on the door. We said, "Who is it?" and some people said, "It's Reality TV."

We let them in too and watched as freaks and geeks were lifted to celebrity status. We watched as cameras followed people around and called it "reality." But whose reality was it anymore?

Later, there was one last knock at the door. We said, "Who is it?" and a crowd said, "It's Stupid and his brother, Tacky, his sister, Inane, his nephew, Shallow, his cousin, Voyeur, and his niece, Crass. Let us in."

And we said, "Sure, what the hell?"

Author Biography

Bill Hanson is a semi-retired voice and network engineer.

Hanson currently lives with his wife in Naples, Florida. They have two sons and a grandson who thinks his grandpa is extremely funny.

Printed in Great Britain
by Amazon

31159632R00066